Promises

of

GOLD

The Legacy of One Woman's Life of Faith Well-Lived

Carol A. Hall

Inviting Developments

SOUTH BRUNSWICK, NEW JERSEY

Published by Inviting Developments, South Brunswick, NJ
For inquiries, email: inviting.developments@gmail.com

Based on a story by Carol Hall, *Promises of Gold* is written in honor of Mary Medford and to the glory of God our Father.

Original cover design by Chloe Hall and summary by Monet Hall
Cover adapted in 2022 for publishing by Lamont Moore
Interior by Rachel L. Hall, Writely Divided

Names have been changed to preserve individual privacy. Quoted text is used to highlight conversations and should not be taken as verbatim.

Scripture quotations, unless otherwise indicated, are taken from the Holy Bible, New International Version®, NIV®. Copyright ©1973, 1978, 1984, 2011 by Biblica, Inc.™ Used by permission of Zondervan. All rights reserved worldwide. www.zondervan.com The "NIV" and "New International Version" are trademarks registered in the United States Patent and Trademark Office by Biblica, Inc.™

Scripture quotations marked (ESV) are from the ESV® Bible (The Holy Bible, English Standard Version®), copyright © 2001 by Crossway, a publishing ministry of Good News Publishers. Used by permission. All rights reserved.

Scripture marked (NKJV) taken from the New King James Version®. Copyright © 1982 by Thomas Nelson. Used by permission. All rights reserved.

ISBN: 979-8-218-03571-6

Advance Praise for *Promises of Gold*

Promises of Gold *is a must read because it shares the story of a phenomenal woman of God who stood the test and believes the word of God. Having faith in the promises of God, she remained stead-fast, unmovable and always abounded in the work of the Lord.*

Be blessed as you read the amazing accounts of Promises of Gold.

Pastor Mary Searight
Abundant Life Family Worship Church

Promises of Gold *is based on a true story of the life of an amazing woman whose faith and love of family is an inspiration to mothers in general and all Christians specifically. I believe that people's lives will be changed and empowered as a result of reading this book. So very proud of her daughter Carol for sharing this story. Well done!*

Donna Soaries
Author of O Lord! Reflections of a Praying Mother

This book is a heart-touching testimony of how a woman's faith helps her overcome hardships and struggles.

Carmen Davila

This book is dedicated to Mary Medford's family
(three daughters and their husbands,
her deceased son and eight grandchildren)
whom she unconditionally loved.

Mary was so grateful to God for her family.

She left a legacy of faith in God
and believed that although there are many bumps
in the road of life,
in faith there is hope and no reason to doubt
that the Lord is God
for He is the Alpha and the Omega
(the beginning and the end)
and He never fails.

Contents

Author's Preface

My mother became more than a parent who gave birth to me on her Christmas birthday and having heard holiday music playing in the delivery room, named me Carol. One day I began to take note of the hundreds of people, young and old, who affectionately called my mother *Mom*. I was taken by her confident persona as I watched her parental and organizational leadership style at home and when heading teams.

As I always gleaned from her resiliency, I was not accustomed to seeing Mommy in despair. On a winter day, I arrived at her apartment at 5:45 p.m. I was welcomed with a heartfelt kiss and alluring aromas. Now, as Mommy was busy in the kitchen, you can imagine the meaningful moment that loomed in my mind when I stumbled across her journal. The scattered notes of moments in her life were contained in a small book. Finding this hidden treasure was like coming across an historical artifact. The evening was not to be another customary drop-in for dinner after a long day of work. It started with a long commute and ended with the beginning of an unforeseen journey.

As I began to read Mommy's journal, I didn't want to believe my eyes. How could such a moral person who dedicated her life to her children, to the point of self-sacrifice, have gone through what she endured? At that moment I had an epiphany, having come to the realization that she, like many people, grieve in silence. It was a heart-wrenching moment of awareness for me. *Why do bad things happen to good people?* was my wailing cry. Compelled to answer this timeless philosophical query, Mommy's notes unveiled a journey of faith in action. I asked myself, *Who goes through hell on earth in complete silence, yet has peace?* Mommy trusted in the God of the biblical scriptures and in faith believed that He is in full operation today, and that belief resulted in a life illuminated with a spirit of hope.

Mommy's inspiring life, in-person storytelling and her journey found in the pages of her journal were the catalyst that drove me to have faith in Jesus Christ and deepened my admiration of her strengths. Compelled by my mother's moral spirit and her love for family, preparation met purpose and united with permission. I was ignited with the idea to write the musical *Promises of Gold*. Thrilled with the heartfelt impact of the musical based on the true story that revealed Mommy's resiliency and faith in God, Mommy and I agreed that the *Promises of Gold* book was a worthy story to be told so that it could encourage its readers.

Mommy's most intimate conversations with me revealed the hardship of tragedy, and the hope of one woman sustained through the revitalizing power of prayer and enriched by God's promises. I was eternally inspired by how she privately held the pain of the past hidden yet close at hand without it negatively impacting her present. As a result, I encouraged Mommy to disrupt the silence. With love for people in mind, she extended her faith-based characteristics to the world.

I believe that in the moment of receiving the *yes* to share a story based on her life, a spiritual bond was unveiled. Through this agreement, I now continue Mommy's lifelong love for people by sharing *Promises of Gold* the book with you.

Take a look into the chapters of *Promises of Gold* and see how the family matriarch, Margaret, like my Mom, is selfless, strong and thoughtful. No matter who you are, you will appreciate the endless sacrifices she made for her family. The way she shows love, patience, kindness and faithfulness is admirable. Her consistent lifestyle is so rewarding to others it easy to adopt Margaret as a role model.

With the rights to write a story based on her life into a musical play first, now the book, with a new musical in the making, the film version of *Promises of Gold* is sure to follow.

As you read *Promises of Gold*, you are invited to open your thoughts and relate to the rollercoaster of life's ups and downs, but more importantly, to be encouraged by Margaret Matias's life of faith enthroned by her belief in God's promises.

This book is written for you, the reader. I pray that after reading *Promises of Gold* you will be inspired to write your journey. I pray you'll experience the joy of sharing words that can encourage someone else. I pray you'll receive a personal release of peace and a sense of resolve to your thoughts.

As I share this narrative based on a true story with you, together let's reap a harvest of closure to the pain of the past, and together rid our souls of every one of our torn emotions so that we can turn toward a future filled with hope and divine purpose.

Throughout my entire life, God has been our family's Savior, Father, Protector and Anchor. I will give Him all the praise and glory forever. His unconditional love, mercy, endless provisions and sufficient grace have sustained us.

When faith is tried during times of trouble, sickness or despair, cry out to God who is the author and finisher of our faith. He hears and cares and will answer in his divine time—the right time. Sometimes He says *yes*, *wait* or *no*, but whatever His answer, we must believe it is for our benefit because God is sovereign.

Carol A. Hall

From the Heart
of Mary Medford

God is a promise keeper and is no respecter of persons (Acts 10:34). What God has done for me can be done for anyone who calls upon His name and believes in Him. In faith, I put my trust in Jesus. He delivered me from unforgettable situations and gave me courage to run the race of life. My hope is in God who has everything in His ultimate, good-willed control. He will do His part; God's divine purpose will prevail. Trust in the good news of Jesus and choose life: one day during a Billy Graham crusade in Barbados I did. That day made all the difference. It allowed me to rise above life's adversities and experience the joy of the Lord as my strength.

Mary Medford (1935–2017)

Then Peter replied, "I now realize how true it is that God does not show favoritism. but accepts from every nation the one who fears him and does what is right. You know the message God sent to the people of Israel, announcing the good news of peace through Jesus Christ, who is Lord of all."

—Acts 10:34–36

Promises

of

GOLD

CHAPTER 1

The Legacy of Loving Determined Women

...I will utter hidden things, things from of old—
things we have heard and known,
things our ancestors have told us.
We will not hide them from their descendants;
we will tell the next generation
the praiseworthy deeds of the LORD,
his power, and the wonders he has done.

—Psalms 78:2–4

My mother's parents were from Guyana, South America. My grandmother, Hannah Campbell, and my great-grandmother, Sophia, were Portuguese. My grandfather Arne, who was from India, migrated to Guyana before marrying Hannah. When my mother and Aunt Grace were very young, their father Arne passed away from pneumonia. On his deathbed, he requested that his wife not remarry. She complied and received his blessing to move the family to Barbados.

This island named Barbados is a picturesque tropical place and is the most southeastern Caribbean island. My grandma Hannah arrived in Barbados from Guyana with her mother, Sophia, and her own two daughters, Luna (my mother) and Grace (my aunt). Soon thereafter, Hannah invented a product called "Frozen Joy." Made from coconuts, this frozen treat-on-a-stick—which resembled today's

Popsicle—quickly became a successful home-based business for Hannah and her mother, who helped her produce it. It was a simple product in concept, but new and innovative for its time.

Hannah and Sophia prepared the Frozen Joy mixture early each morning. First, they pierced the three dark, round, knuckle-sized eyes of the coconuts and poured off the juice, or "milk." Then they would crack the hard, brown, dry, straw-like covered shell exposing the "meat," or white portion, of the coconut that was then separated from the shell and grated. Next, they used a piece of white cotton to strain the rest of the juice from the finely grated meat. This was done repeatedly until all the juice was extracted. It was a very time-consuming process. Next they combined these two ingredients and divided the mixture so it could be flavored with vanilla, chocolate, cherry or mango. Finally, they formed it around sticks and set it to freeze in their ice box. Once frozen, the ice pops were carefully placed in trays and stored inside portable ice boxes that were equipped with wheels, which allowed hired salespeople to roll the product to the various schools and sell it to the children. Kids would line up each day to spend two pence to purchase a Frozen Joy. My grandmother and great-grandmother contributed much support to the family with the lucrative profits from the sales.

Once home from school, Luna and Grace looked forward to enjoying extras of the delicious ice pops that hadn't been sold. The young salespeople made sure to return from work each afternoon with at least one Frozen Joy pop each for Luna and Grace. Their goal, my mother told me, was to always stay in their mother Hannah's good graces in order to receive an ice pop! Proud to have a mother who created popsicles and eager to please Hannah as a result, Luna rehearsed lines from a popular song, "Ramona," which recounted dreading the dawn and waking up in the morning to find the person gone.

Having a heart of gold, one afternoon Hannah was helping an old, crippled man who lived next door. Luna was waiting patiently in Hannah's work area for the reward of good behavior. With the idea of surprising Hannah, Luna wrote the words to "Ramona" in Hannah's accounting book. In that moment, she noticed that the family was doing very well and so Luna looked forward to a bright financial future—that is, until a rude awakening of the new dawn came.

Sometimes great-grandma Sophia allowed my mother, Luna and aunt Grace to sleep with her. That gave time for each girl to tell their grandma Sophia all about her exciting day at school. Great-grandma Sophia used these evenings to encourage and teach Mommy and Aunt Grace poems. She did it with love, and laughter was always heard late into the night. It was a familiar sound within the household, like a crackling toasty fireplace that spread warmth throughout the home.

The next morning, as was her custom, my great-grandmother Sophia arose to wake entrepreneur grandma Hannah so they could start the day's task of preparing the custard to make the Frozen Joys. Entering Hannah's bedroom, Sophia reached out to touch her and was shocked to realize her daughter was dead. She had died during the night of unknown causes. Being a young lady with teenaged children, Hannah's death paralyzed the household. No one ever discovered what caused her sudden death. Shock and disbelief reigned, and for a long time Aunty Grace and my mother Luna, at ages thirteen and fourteen respectively, would share hugs and good memories of Grandma Hannah before going to bed most nights.

Around the year 1930, it was very difficult for my great-grandmother Sophia to carry on. She made plans to shut down the Frozen Joy business. With the sole responsibility to raise her great-grandchildren, Sophia felt she could not proceed with the business after the death of her daughter. Aunt Grace and Mommy tried to help Sophia each morning, but her level of energy was never the same after Hannah's death. She gradually allowed the business to fail. Then, barely a year later, the angel of death revisited their home. Great-grandmother Sophia died, leaving Luna and aunt Grace, still young girls, to fend for themselves.

Prior to her death, Sophia had hired an attorney to handle all the business affairs. Since great-grandma Sophia did not have any living, known adult relatives to help, she relied upon the advice of the attorney exclusively. Now, upon her death, neither Luna nor Grace knew anything about the financial affairs of the home or the complexity of accounting and financial paperwork. So, when Sophia's attorney arrived on the scene to take over the financial affairs, they could only hope that he was treating them fairly. As it happened, he was not. At first, it seemed as if all was well. The attorney arranged to provide Luna and Grace with a small monthly stipend until they reached the age where they could live on their own. But in the process, he slyly embezzled most of the money grandma Hannah and great-grandmother Sophia had saved from the Frozen Joy business. From the remaining funds, the girls were able to buy a small house together, but the rest of the business earnings disappeared with the dishonest attorney. Aunt Grace decided at age 21 to go back to her native land of Guyana. That left Luna in Barbados. Luna had married Miles, my father, as it was customary then to marry at a young age. From this union, my mother Luna seemed to conceive a baby almost every year. At about age 36, she had given birth to a total of twelve children, of which three died as infants.

CHAPTER 2

Beautiful Barbados Beginnings

"For I know the plans I have for you," declares the LORD,
"plans to prosper you and not to harm you,
plans to give you hope and a future."

—Jeremiah 29:11

I was born on the beautiful island of Barbados in December 1935. As a child, I would stand on the jagged coastal rocks and shield my eyes from the piercing sun as I gazed into the distance of the blue tranquil waters that surrounded the island. On days when a cool breeze would blow, I would reach out as if to catch hold of it, then whimsically place it in my pocket. Small, yet rich in culture, the island of Barbados awakens every sense with its breathtaking displays of golden sandy-white beaches. The temperature rests near 88 degrees most days, and captivating sunsets slowly move in during the evenings. When the sun decides to leave the day behind, it colors the night sky with shades of amber and burnt orange, with shades of topaz reflecting onto the blue ocean.

Barbados, my birth home, consists of eleven communities called parishes, each named after an apostle of the Catholic faith, except for a parish in our southern region known as Christ Church. The island is endowed with natural breathtaking landscapes and friendly people. In my opinion, it is one of the most stunning of all the hidden treasures of the earth. It's no wonder England desired to rule the island of Barbados from 1627 until Barbadians gained emancipation in 1834. On November 30, 1966, they declared their independence.

With a diversity of settlers through the years, native Barbadians, or Bajans, today present a range of skin tones, eye colors and hair textures. When I look at my family and through pictures of my ancestors, I can easily trace the ethnic overlap in my blood: Irish, East Indian, Portuguese and most probably African. I am a mixture of them all.

Bridgetown, the capitol of economic activity in Barbados, was not very far from where my family lived in Bank Hall, St. Michael, one of the parishes I so fondly called home. Each morning on my way to school, I walked the stony paths and narrow roads lined with cascades of tropical plants whose flowers danced in the light breeze and warm sunshine.

Our home was small in size, simple in décor and built of wood. With their carefully assembled furniture, the bedrooms consisted of the basics: a bed, a side table and a wooden cabinet for clothing. An ordinary brass lamp was used on very dark nights when our opulent moon dims. My parents' room had a rocking chair that Mommy frequently used to lull us children to sleep on hot, restless nights. The windows of our home welcomed the visiting winds and framed a picture-like view of our cherished garden and livestock. Family life was the joy of our existence and the laughter we shared better than medicine. Somewhat traditional, our family unit consisted of a full-time working father and a stay-at-home mother who consistently met daily domestic challenges with grace and kindness. With a limited amount of resources, my mother faced every new day with her sweet spirit and without complaint. My mother was a godly woman who taught me how to pray by example. Unlike other parents who would harshly scold their children, saying things like, "Behave! Wunna want a backhand lash? If you don't listen, you will feel!", my mother was very caring when needing to be stern.

Perhaps because some lived there all their lives, many Barbadians take for granted all that the small island has to offer. Yet those who visit often loathe leaving. I remember the times when I sat on the beach and reflected on God's handiwork and His great power that had created it all. My heart would swell within me as I felt so very close to the one who had formed it all. In those moments, in the silence of my thanksgiving, I was often transported to a tranquil time and place of absolute beauty, a vision and place I clung to and savored—until I would arise with reluctance to relish the warm, powdery sand that filled the recesses between my toes.

Barbados has been known for having some of the purest water in the world. The rainwater is filtered naturally through God's strategically placed coral filters, like a special fountain created just for the island. We did not have the luxury of running water. Only the wealthy were fortunate enough to have indoor plumbing. Our "toilet" was enclosed in an outdoor shed modernly known as an outhouse. The wooden enclosure stood about five feet in height with a door that latched on the inside. A simple hole was dug deep into the ground to capture excretions. It was something I wanted to forget as my least-invited friend of nature, the lizard, would climb out of the hole when I'd least expect it. There is nothing worse than being startled by a crawling lizard while in the process of relieving yourself. As I grew older, I vowed that one day I would move into a house with proper plumbing.

To meet the family's water requirements, my father hired a man from our neighborhood to fill a huge wooden barrel with water for us every other day. In the early morning, with an empty bucket in each hand, he would trot back and forth along the worn path and return with the buckets full, careful not to spill a drop of the water needed for cooking, washing and bathing. For his labor, our neighbor was paid twelve coppers (one shilling) a week. Water was also needed to quench the thirst of the fruits and vegetables as well as the livestock. The water troughs were filled daily with carefully measured portions to satisfy the needs of our Black Belly goats, pigs, chickens, pigeons, etc.

The assistance of the midwife was important to the expansion of the family, since it was customary to have babies at home. My mother's midwife was a tall, brown-skinned woman with brunette-colored hair. While polite and respectful, the midwife didn't say much to us children when she came to our home to deliver a baby. She reserved her few words to comfort my mother and prepare for delivery.

The topic of sex was taboo for children and was not discussed within the household. Mommy, as a caring, godly woman, told me that until I was "old enough," I was not allowed to speak to boys and definitely was not allowed to sit on their laps. If I did, she said, I would surely become pregnant! Parents felt that children did not need to know the details of childbirth (after all, it was a time in history when children were expected to be seen and not heard). Each time my mother had a new baby, the nurse arrived, always with her suitcase in tow. Not surprisingly, with no other information to go by, we children came to believe that any new brother or sister came from the midwife's large suitcase.

On one occasion, we were celebrating the birth of yet another newborn sibling when I noticed the midwife was not there to share in the light meal which consisted of cheese cutters (soft, round rolls the size of the palm of your hand), Barbados cheese (a white-colored Australian brand sharp cheese sold in various size blocks), and a cool pitcher of Mauby drink. The drink is made from the bark of a tree found in the Caribbean well-known for its health attributes. The bark is steeped in hot water to draw out its strong, bitter taste. The tea is then generously sweetened with cane sugar then chilled before serving. Desert was often a very thick, heavily sweetened milk liberally spread over slices of bread. Naturally, I was puzzled because the midwife was not at the house. I could ask no one at home how the baby got here—so I escaped the festivities to run over to our neighbor, Ms. Melissa. I asked her the great secret question: "Where do babies come from?"

Ms. Melissa was a friendly lady who worked in the outdoor marketplace. She sold all types of freshly grown produce from her vendor cart. On my way home from school, Ms. Melissa would make it a point to be cordial and she would invite me to take mangos from her tree home to my family. With her comforting voice, light complexion and long hair, Ms. Melissa would take a rest from the morning's gardening by lethargically soaking in the sun from her veranda. I did not let Mommy know of my secret meetings with Ms. Melissa. Conversations with Ms. Melissa were very enjoyable. For some reason I always felt confident that she told me the truth, no matter what the question. So, on this day, I ran to her to inquire about the origins of the new baby.

Ms. Melissa encouraged me not to tell my siblings as they were too young to understand. I promised never to tell anyone, not even my other sisters or brothers. I was shocked to find out that babies came from Mommy's body. Although Mommy's belly was big, the suitcase myth had been quite compelling. After this, I dared not ask how the baby got inside the belly to start with.

As a young child, I had the duty of caring for my younger siblings. As the eldest girl, I took on the task of being fourth in command to assist my parents. There was no time for extensive training, but thankfully, I could mimic the roles performed by my parents in many aspects. I rolled up my sleeves and took charge in areas of cleaning and cooking, and I reinforced my parents' rules. We were a family of nine children: six girls and three boys.

Taking care of my younger siblings was a challenge that required patience and love. They were at various stages of growth, with some already walking and others just beginning. All needed individual attention and love. I was not afraid. I understood my responsibility—to help shape the future of my siblings by teaching, first by example and eventually by delegation.

My sisters were so much fun. Though Paris, Jennifer and I looked different from each other, it was clear that we came from the same parents. Jennifer and Paris had long, flowing, black wavy hair and light caramel complexions with dark brown eyes, all features from our mom. I had thick hair with a dark reddish tone, and, like my youngest sister, I had green eyes and a lighter complexion, like my father's mother.

We did not have much, but we had each other. The bond of love set the foundation for the family lineage. At the dawn of each new day, I attempted to comb my sisters' hair into two simple plaits. One by one, I separated their curly hair down the center from the crown to the nape. The trick was to use water along with pomade to help set and hold their braided hair. I held each plat stationary by tying it with a ribbon. Each plat was intertwined by three sections of hair to create a neat balance of texture. By the end of the day, with us all romping outside in the garden, our braids would come undone, revealing a beautiful pattern of waves that flowed down our backs. After a yawn or two, my tired young siblings were more than ready to take their baths and get ready for bed.

I was in charge of bathing them all. I used a large enough basin that would hold two or three of the little ones at the same time. Despite the playing, I still managed to get everyone clean with our "blue soap" made from coconut oil, lye and fruit extract. Bath time was always a messy, wet experience, but fun for all—even me! I'm still amazed that after doing my required chores, I was also able to meet my school studies. No matter how late, I made sure to complete my assignments and prepare my clothes for the next day.

Overall, I was a happy young girl. I did not despair at having so many adult responsibilities to fill my childhood. Often, at night, I would go outside to look up into the dark sky to admire our clear, bright moon and myriad stars. I recall one special night, though, when it all suddenly seemed different—stronger, brighter, closer and somehow more reassuring. The moon appeared to be unusually large that evening and so close to the earth that I felt I could almost reach out and touch it. Overwhelmed with emotion, I sat down on the grass and just smiled. In that sparkling moment, I thought about my loving family and was grateful.

CHAPTER 3

Home Sweet Home

Honor your father and your mother,
so that you may live long in the land
the LORD your God is giving you.

—Exodus 20:12

A s a child, my daily existence was simple, but as part of a large family my days were frequently jam-packed. Once home from school, I always started chores immediately. My mother had her hands full and needed all the help I could provide. Almost each year the family was expanding. By the time I was eighteen, my mother had given birth to twelve children. My responsibilities included making sure all the siblings were settled and had something to snack on before I began the process of washing diapers—it seemed there were always babies in our household and disposable diapers were items as yet un-dreamed of! In Barbados, the sun was still high at 3:00 p.m., so it was a great time for washing and hanging the clothes. It was my job to soak the dirty diapers in a large pail of soapy water. As taught by my mother, I added baking soda to the detergent to help remove the yel-low and brown stains. Next to the soaking bucket sat a smaller one which I filled with clean rinse water. I repeated the soaking and rins-ing process until all the diapers were bright white and clean, then hung them on the clothesline that stretched across our fence-enclosed back yard. By morning, the diapers were dry, fresh and ready to be dirtied again. It seemed a never-ending chore, but it was absolutely necessary for the welfare of my younger siblings and it was a great help to my mother, so I didn't complain.

During her later child-bearing years, Mommy gradually needed more and more assistance and was often unable to participate in our family rituals, such as meal preparation. Over the years, she had gradually developed a severe case of rheumatoid arthritis. This paralyzing disease did not allow her to cook as frequently as she once had. She became unable to do chores around the house, so she delegated these responsibilities to my brother and me. I did all I could to help ease Mommy's pain, which eventually kept her confined to a chair or her bed for most of the day. The swelling of her joints was so intense that sometimes just feeding herself was a great challenge. The twisted bones in her hands caused her hands to clench like the fists of a newborn baby, and her feet were so painfully enlarged that it was difficult for her to wear shoes. Unable to access needed medical support due to limited finances at the time, Mommy would smile and try to endure the excruciating pain. Her only relief came from taking aspirin, which was the only medicine available to her. Some days the soreness within her joints was so unbearable that she would confine herself to the darkness of her room. She was reluctant to come out. We could hear her slowly rocking in her chair and weeping.

I believe Mommy was not interested in showing defeat to her family, as she strived to be the epitome of motherhood and had always been determined to teach us to be strong and stalwart. She felt that to bow to her pain in front of her children might diminish the example she had set for us. Above all, she clung to her hopes and dreams for the success of her children and their children to follow.

In spite of her physical ailments, I considered my mother Luna to be truly beautiful on the inside and out. She had shiny black hair: it was beautiful to behold when the cool evening breeze ruffled those long wavy strands. She had beautiful warm eyes and caramel colored skin. I had always enjoyed greeting my mother with a big hug. Her skin was soft as petals in the dew of the morning. It was sad to see her change as her illness crept upon her—and sadder, still, that because she was so fragile and pain-ridden, I had to be careful to hug her ever so gently. What I really wanted to do was throw my arms around her and hug her tightly to comfort her from the pain.

No matter what happened, though, Mommy's faith sustained her. My mother was Roman Catholic, a godly woman who knew how to pray. I recall many times when Mommy would have me stop whatever I was doing to take a moment to say our Hail Mary prayers together with rosary beads in hand. She was sincere about thanking God for that which we had been given. Mommy was a soft-spoken, kind and loving woman who never raised her voice, yet she was a firm disciplinarian. If we misbehaved, and she gave us a look, we understood immediately that we were to stop whatever we were doing—even if we weren't always sure what we had done wrong. Sometimes, though, my brothers needed more than a warning glance. They were "hard ears." As some Bajans say: "Hard ears don't hear, you know." Although they needed a scolding, Mommy had a way of approaching discipline in a loving tone that in return caused us to move to action.

I cherish the memory of how, sometimes, she would turn to me and give me a big hug just when I needed it most. The look in her eyes told me no matter what happened in life, I was loved. Now, perhaps she gave that same look to all my brothers and sisters. And perhaps we were all her favorites, at one time or another. I am sure Mommy would have denied that she ever had favorites among us, if we had asked.

***

My father, Miles, was a slim, handsome man. His skin was a light tan color that was deeper still as a result of his spending many of his youthful days playing in the sun. Athletic, Daddy was proud of his physique. Rugged in stature at around 6'2", he usually commanded the attention of every one in a room with his bright white smile. When asked a question, he characteristically paused before answering. When he finally answered, he never mumbled or rambled on with long sentences. Daddy was clear and to the point, and he was a hardworking man who cared for his family. As I grew older and curious about the attributes of love and relationships, I avoided asking

Daddy questions for fear that he might one day use the warden's long, six inch wide staff, holstered in his belt, to discipline me at the thought of the opposite sex.

Daddy carried the long wooden baton as a warden at the prison, which was a massive compound. And from what I understand it was rare to find people who were punished for murder during this era as this type of crime was rare in Barbados. Children were taught to respect the prison officers and, unlike today, would never dream of speaking to them or about them in a rude manner. Daddy didn't have many friends apart from a few men who worked at the prison. They served as his drinking buddies at the local bar.

Daddy did his best to be a loving father and a hardworking provider, but in my eyes, he at times fell short in a particular area that I have kept secret for many years. A strong but loving fatherly role model has historically said to be an important key in the growth and development of a child's life, and I believe my father lived up to this expectation in many ways. I knew Daddy loved us children, but to me he was extremely strict, sometimes frighteningly so. I often wondered if he created that hard external image to protect himself at work and was unable to turn it off when he came home, or if it was truly his nature no matter where he was or what he was doing.

Along with the exacting demands of his personality, he was a man who expected excellence. Everything must be in its place without his asking. The home should be clean at all times, regardless that it was the abode of so many active children. From time to time, my father pitched in to help clean and sometimes cook a meal, but those days most of the time it was me or Mommy who did the work of the home.

I never quite understood a certain type of love from Daddy, yet I treated him with honor and respect. My choices in life were greatly affected by how I expected Daddy to react to them. I know his possible reaction affected my dating decisions. Boys were not allowed to come into the home when they'd come to visit me. Daddy was very clear on this rule. When I was finally allowed to have a boyfriend, Daddy sat on one side of our enclosed porch and my date and I sat on the other, our chairs across from his. Daddy did not speak much to my guest but only sat there in his oversized wooden chair with his legs crossed, smoking his cigarette and staring at my friend. He seemed to me like a lion waiting to pounce on his prey. Nor did Daddy leave until my friend had made his proper goodbyes. At the time, I desperately wished Daddy would not sit on the porch, the constant chaperone. But part of me understood that this was his way of showing me how much he cared for my well-being, my safety and my reputation.

I do remember some special moments with Daddy, mainly to do with music. Daddy was a musician. When he was home on weekends, he sometimes gathered us around, played the piano and sang a variety of different tunes. His beautiful, full baritone voice rang through the house like a conga drum echoing from somewhere deep in a rain forest—pure and steady. We often sang along. Though he seldom expressed unguarded emotions to those around him, sometimes Daddy would sing to the babies while rocking them to sleep.

When it comes to music, it is easy to distinguish a Barbadian from a native of another Caribbean island. The sing-song tones of Barbadians are warm and sweet. I loved to watch Daddy during these wonderful bonding moments. It was this musical side of Daddy that convinced me that this was a way he showed his love.

His appreciation for music led him to compose tunes of his own, including a beautiful love song that he titled "When the Waves Kiss the Sand." He had great hopes of someday recording some of his songs professionally. With prompting from his friends and family, he sent some of his lyrics to music producers in the United States. Even though the producers claimed never to have received his music or lyrics, years later we heard that his music was published and recorded by another artist in America. Sadly, while his music fueled the dreams of someone else, Daddy's own dream never became a reality.

CHAPTER 4

Why Me Too?

Fathers, do not provoke your children to anger,
but bring them up in the discipline and instruction of the Lord.

—Ephesians 6:4 (ESV)

D addy said one afternoon when I was nine years old, "Today is such a beautiful day, you should pack your towel and bathing suit and we can go play on the beach away from the crowds. This is a nice time of year. I can teach you to swim. Just the two of us—the king and his beautiful princess."

I was so excited! Finally, I would spend time alone with Daddy. With the constant demands of helping Mommy in the home, I almost never had time for myself, much less an opportunity to spend time with my father. His patriarchal expectations had kept me at arm's reach and on guard all the years of my youth. I always had to get chores done in a timely and exacting fashion and never leave any task forgotten, or I'd risk Daddy's disapproval.

Now, on this glorious, sunny day, it was actually Daddy who was suggesting I forego an afternoon at home, where I would undoubtedly have found some task that needed doing, and take to the beach with him for the afternoon to relax in the sun and perhaps have a long chatty talk. I was so excited, I thought to myself that Daddy must be taking me to the beach as a post-ninth birthday gift. So with great joy, I ran to my room to get my things. A towel, change of clothes and my sandals were quickly packed. With the beach a few miles away from our home located in St. Michael, I decided to put on my bathing suit at the house so that once I arrived at the beach, I could quickly remove my pink, floral, cotton bodice and gathered matching skirt and run straight into the refreshing ocean.

On the way out, I stopped in Mommy's room to tell her of my expedition. She shared her motherly advice: "Be careful, sweetie. You know I do not like the beach. The water is the mouth of the grave." This was the first time I had ever seen fear in my mother's eyes, and it puzzled me. She looked as if she had something more to say, but when she did not speak, I bade her goodbye for the afternoon and ran to join Daddy outside.

***

When the shore was in sight, I picked up my pace and began to skip while Daddy walked to the beach. At that point, I was practically pulling Daddy as we held hands, laughing together and burying our toes into the soft Barbados sand until our feet touched the warm water. I noticed the sun was almost touching the horizon. It was later in the day than I realized, and I noticed then that the beach was empty of other sunbathers and swimmers. But I didn't care—in fact, I was glad. It felt almost as if Daddy and I were royalty, enjoying our own private island. As I looked around to determine the best place to settle, Daddy signaled that we set up camp near the large rocks close to the shoreline. I spread my blanket, then pulled off my bodice and skirt. In my blue bathing suit, I ran out to enjoy the ocean waves. Daddy removed his vest shirt to catch the fading rays of sunlight, but did not go for a swim in the water. He remained seated by the rocks, wearing his dark sunglasses and slowly smoking a cigarette while he sipped his Guinness beer.

After swimming around a while in the still, blue waters that softly splashed against the rocks, I returned to the blanket to play in the sand. "Come here, let me dry you off." My father's command was delivered in the same deep, hollow tones that when uttered at home meant he would not brook any disobedience.

Startled, I obeyed and turned to allow Daddy to towel the dripping water from my shoulders and back. Suddenly, his tone shifted as he expressed his love for me and appreciation for all I do. "Margaret, your green eyes are more beautiful than any emerald stone and they glisten more brightly than any star in the black clear sky. I love you more than words could ever say." Then he gently turned me around and slowly pulled me toward him and gave me a hug. Ever so quietly, he told me to lie down on the towel. Though confused, I instinctively obeyed his familiar, comforting tone of command. This was my father after all. What daughter does not want to be daddy's little girl? As the second oldest child, I was glad that Daddy loved me. I had always trusted him and never, ever disobeyed him.

To my surprise, he also dropped to the sand. He immediately began to caress my arms with tanning oil, then gently massaged it into my shoulders. I was not sure what to think as I had never had so much tanning oil on me before.

"Margaret, after all the hard work you do in the home, you deserve to be treated like a princess." Then, carefully pulling down the straps from my one piece bathing suit, Daddy gave me a belly rub.

I giggled as if he were intentionally tickling me. "Daddy, what are you doing? That tickles!"

He placed his pointer finger at his lips and silently whispered for me to hush, as if there were people nearby, but I was sure most were celebrating the happenings around the Crop Over season (the traditional harvest festival).

It was so hard not to burst out in a hysterical laugh as he oiled my hips and caressed my inner thighs, legs and wiggled my toes while giving me the biggest smile I ever experienced. Reminding me how beautiful I was and how much he loved me, Daddy crawled his fingers back up my legs. One hand oiled my chest and the other found its way to places that my instincts felt were wrong for oiling. Then, unexpectedly, he placed his massive body on top of my frail, nine-year-old, well-oiled frame. For a moment, he looked down into my eyes, then said, "Don't make a sound."

I was very frightened, but was more terrified to scream. His breath smelled of the beer he was drinking, and I suddenly recalled that he had already been drinking before we left home. But what was he doing? What was happening? The weight of his body felt as if it were pushing all the air from my lungs. Perturbed, I was gasping for air. Fear and confusion engulfed me as I tried to speak.

"Please stop!" I really wanted him to stop.

"Don't make a sound," he repeated.

Held down and in utter shock, I could not breathe well and was becoming weak and panicked.

"Don't be afraid. I will not hurt you."

But it did hurt me. "What are you doing?" I cried as a rush of tears filled my eyes. "Stop! Please stop!" I could barely squeeze out the words. Then I realized that I had not spoken at all. My words were only inside my head. I had not the breath to utter them aloud. Daddy's implied threat that I be quiet made me truly frightened to make a sound, even if I could have.

I could hardly believe what was happening, and I knew even less what I could do to stop it. This was my father! I was not as strong as he was, I was not brave in the face of his authority and I had barely the air or strength to sob, much less to call out. Besides, the beach and especially where we were near the rocks was empty when we arrived and it remained so for the duration of this nightmare of a moment.

Horrified, I realized that perhaps Daddy had planned this all along. Perhaps this was why he had waited until so late in the day to suggest our beach trip. The possibility confused and frightened me even further.

Unable to do anything to help myself, I lay stiff and frozen, shivering against the still-warm sand, immobile as one of the mud pie dolls I had formed earlier when playing with my younger siblings. I was only nine. As my father did what he liked with me—apparently drunk and oblivious to any pain he might be inflicting—I tried to project my mind far away, to think of anything else but what was happening to me. Pain-launched tears rolled down from the corners of my eyes to pool in my ears and puddle on the sand. My small whimpers were lost in the crashing boom of the waves against the large black rocks. "Please stop" were the words resounding inside my mind, but it was impossible to scream.

He suddenly let out a loud sound and rolled over and away from me. As soon as I could safely get up, I was on my feet and was hurting in more ways than one. Not concerned whether or not daddy would miss me, I wiped myself off with a towel and grabbed my clothes to get dressed and I ran fast, so desperately fast that, for once in my life, I felt I might actually get home to Mommy ahead of the wind. However, my ordeal had sucked most of my strength from my limbs and with my newly experienced fatigue the already lengthy distance from home felt more like a hike. Once my anxiety-induced adrenaline slightly rescinded and with home in mind, my steps became more weighted, to the point of slowing to a stumble. Then, in utter physical and mental anguish, I wrapped my arms around my body as if to hold myself together from breaking. I was moving slowly toward home when I decided to stop in the marketplace to rest.

My roiling thoughts were nearly unbearable. What had happened to me? Why had Daddy done this to me? Was there something wrong with me that I deserved such treatment? I did not understand. I just did not understand. He said he loved me. Tears streamed down my cheeks afresh.

I imagined the conversation I needed to have with my mother once I arrived home. The scene might look like this: Still in my bathing suit, I'd run crying into her room and throw myself into her arms. "What happened, sweetie? What is all the fuss?" she would ask, hugging me tight. I'd pull back to look in her eyes and would see that same look she had given me before I left with Daddy for the beach. Suddenly I wondered if she had somehow known what had been about to happen to me. Regardless, I had to tell her—I had to practice saying it out loud to make it real, or I might come to disbelieve it myself. It still seemed like such an unreal moment, a nightmare that I should have awakened from but couldn't. In that imagined moment, I opened my mouth to tell my mother what had happened to me at the hands of my own father, and suddenly I could not speak. How could I tell my mother about the things my daddy had done to me?

What if she didn't believe me? She would be torn between her beloved husband and her beloved daughter. Her loyalties would be tested to the extreme, but as a faithful Roman Catholic wife, her marriage vows had to be honored, so what could she say? With whom could she side? In a flash, I imagined my sweet mother turning into a monster with repulsion toward me: "Child, you listen to me, and you listen good. Don't you ever talk such foolishness about your father! He would never do such a thing! He loves you. He loves his children, and he would never do such a thing to any one of them. Now, if you got yourself in trouble with some young fast boy down at the beach, then that is because you are loose! You need to slow down your fresh tail and cover yourself up. Look what you have on! You look like a nasty street girl. I am ashamed of you!"

The mother I loved would never think these things of me, nor say them to me, either. Nevertheless, in my brokenhearted state, I had almost begun to conjure up such things of myself. Was it my fault? Was my simple blue bathing suit really as indecent as it suddenly felt? If these things weren't true, then why had my dad felt it was all right to take such liberties with me, his own daughter?

I never wanted to hear such accusations come from my mother's lips, so rather than take the chance, I prepared in my mind to cover my distress in advance of arriving home. Besides, there was also the implied threat from my father that I should keep quiet or else. Though I had run away too quickly for him to warn me not to tell anyone what he'd done, I knew my silence was expected. His unspoken command was just as incontrovertible as any words he might ever say aloud. He knew it and I knew it, and I don't think it ever crossed his mind to worry that he might be discovered in his sin. From that moment on, I was truly afraid of Daddy and hated what had been done to me with every fiber of my soul.

As time went on, I had even more reason to feel this way as he would nauseatingly filter his actions behind words of love, adoration and acceptance to the point of normalcy. After years of the same treatment, the pure, unadulterated understanding of love between Daddy and me was forever tarnished. I had become a surrogate wife and was deeply sad for my mommy who morally loved us unconditionally. I did not know if she knew about Daddy's shenanigans, but I was not going to be the one to break her kind heart given her waning health.

The next time I saw Daddy, I avoided him to the best of my ability. But it made no difference. He knew that no matter what he did to me, nothing would happen to him. No one would believe me I thought. Even if I told the truth, my father would somehow surely invoke his charm and charisma to exonerate himself and shift the blame. The pain of his loving tenderness and violations continued and erupted into what I consider a deep, dark shameful secret, memories too unwarranted to share.

CHAPTER 5

My Father's Lineage

Children's children are a crown to the aged,
and parents are the pride of their children.

—Proverbs 17:6

*E*ach year I looked forward to my vacation. When the last school bell of the last school day of the year rang out, my friends and I would rush outside, eager to taste our long anticipated freedom from schoolbooks and homework and knuckle-rapping teachers.

Even though island life in those days was generally mundane, my friends and I always managed to have fun. With no radio, television or computer, as well as the absence of toys, we instead played games similar to hopscotch and pick-ups, using smooth pebbles from the beach as our tokens. Our homemade dolls became characters within our storybook families, for which we invented whole lives. We "cooked" for our storybook families, too, creating mud pies that we sprinkled with grated coconut before leaving them in the sun to "bake." Although my siblings and I enjoyed the days when we played in the sand, some of our vacation was often spent at my grandmother's house.

Of Irish descent, my father's mother, Grandma Maya Earthman Tanner, was a petite woman of about 5 feet 4 inches who weighed about 145 pounds. She had green eyes – a color I inherited – and a fair complexion. From my earliest memories, she had long, beautiful, silver hair. After Daddy's father died, she had remarried to a man we called Papa Tanner. Grandma was a skilled dressmaker. Many children of her time learned how to cut, mend and hand sew clothing – but Grandma was an artist. She often sewed our uniforms for school. My father Miles was Grandma Tanner's favorite child. Uncle Avery lived nearby, so I suppose he was liked second. From what I understand, Daddy had other siblings who lived far away, but I didn't know them. Daddy had always been kind and helpful to his mother and often helped around the house. In turn, Grandma did not hesitate to voice her opinions about Mommy – no one ever seemed good enough for her Miles. This made more sense when I was older and learned that my grandmother had hoped Miles would delay getting married so that he would be at home with her for a while longer, to help her with the multitude of chores and maintenance on their land. When Daddy and Mommy became engaged, Grandma Tanner made no secret of the fact that she considered the two of them too young to be married. When they eventually married, Mommy was in her late teens. As the years passed, Grandma's feelings did not change – unless it was for the worse. She clearly did not like Mommy. Experiencing this type of tension made it difficult to be happy when we were allowed to visit. "You're lucky, you know," Grandma Tanner once told her, "you caught a good man. Take care of my son, you hear me?"

My grandmother's house was the largest I had ever seen in my young life. In my childish inexperience, I was sure it was a mansion. The first thing I would notice when approaching the house was the great veranda that extended all the way around it. After walking up three steps to the porch, I would pass through a large white door that opened to a big living room reserved for special guests. The furniture in the living room was of fine mahogany, with many different drawers and compartments adorned with polished brass handles. Each of the room's windows were framed by sheer white curtains draped "just right." The shutters that opened and closed at the flip of a lever perfectly enhanced the sun's warming rays as they glistened and seeped through the windows. From the living room, I would proceed into the parlor, where more informal visiting was conducted. On the parlor wall hung a giant clock with a steadily swinging pendulum. When the long hands of the clock face converged each new hour, a deep chime rang out to confirm that time had moved on.

My grandmother's home was one of the first in the area to have indoor plumbing. Whenever I visited, I especially looked forward to using the "water toilet" located in its own separate room. This was always my first stop! From there, I would go down the hallway to discover the true center of Grandma's home: her bedroom. It was strictly off limits to the children. Nevertheless, I got a good look at it once or twice. It was a clean, simple and uncluttered room, without the mementos one usually finds in a personal space. Grandma enjoyed her private reading time in the evening. It allowed her to escape from the day-to-day moments of her chores and the responsibilities of running a household. Down a long hallway were three other moderately decorated bedrooms which Grandma kept clean and furnished in case family members came to visit. My siblings and I shared these three rooms when we stayed with Grandma.

Grandma had a very large cast iron stove in the backyard, like the one at my own house. She also had an ice box inside the house that kept her food fresh – an uncommon luxury at that time. It was used to store meats for extended periods of time. This was very handy, since Grandma only needed to prepare small meals whenever we were not visiting her.

Behind the house was a large plot of land where, for many years, Grandma raised a festival of vegetables and fruits including luscious mango and avocado trees. Each season, she would share the bounty with her neighbors and with Daddy and us grandchildren.

Grandma was a generous woman and she seemed to like us grandchildren — as long as we were not under foot or misbehaving. When we visited, she was clearly uncomfortable with our loud noises and the fast movements and messes we made. Children were not allowed to run around in her home, as it was kept in mint condition and she wanted it to stay just so. When we were not sent outside to play, Grandma would have us sit still whenever we were inside the house. Summer vacation seemed to come to a halt for us grandchildren once we were indoors at Grandma's house.

I never knew Grandma Tanner's first husband since he died when my father was young. My grandmother later remarried a man with the last name of Tanner. He worked at the docks where the ships came in. Every day, he would transport loads of sugar that were picked up from the sugarcane refinery and loaded onto the export boats. Granddaddy Tanner was much older than Grandma. He had thin grey hair and wore glasses that seemed permanently affixed on top of his nose. From his many years of working under the blazing tropical sun and in and around the salty waters, the lines around his eyes and mouth had flowed into a permanent frown. Unlike my daddy's father, Granddaddy Tanner was a short man, only 5 foot 2, and very portly. His large belly was the result of the many nights he and his fellow shipmates lounged and drank after a long day of work. That was his nightly routine, almost a sacrament. Even late in his life, when many of his friends had moved away or died, he continued his late-night drinking.

Granddaddy Tanner seemed to me to be a mysterious man. He was lord and master of his home, and he decided whether or not someone could come into his house. I noticed only a few of his friends ever stayed for lengthy visits. He was very distant with us children. I later realized that he may have been at least part of the reason Grandma Tanner treated us as she did during our school break visits. While we were indoors, she may have wanted to make sure Mr. Tanner wasn't disturbed by our presence.

Grandma had been married only eight years when Mr. Tanner (Papa) was killed accidentally by a machine at the sugarcane factory where he worked. His passing left her alone in a big empty house. It was more than she could maintain properly by herself. Until that point, she always had someone to depend on, someone to take care of her. But now her second husband was gone and Grandma's physical ailments prevented her from planting her garden and tending it the way she and Mr. Tanner had together.

I never really knew what was on Grandma's mind, as she didn't share her thoughts with us youngsters. But as the years marched on, she became more and more bitter — like a lemon that when left unsqueezed grows rancid and unpalatable. So, despite the luxuries of Grandma's "mansion," our visits to her home eventually began to pall for us as well as for her. Regardless of the fascination we originally felt with Grandma Tanner's home, there finally came a day when Mommy thought it in our best interest to no longer visit.

I have sometimes wondered why Grandma, with all her apparent wealth and convenience, became so unhappy. Perhaps she missed doing all the lively things she had done before her physical ailments slowed her down. Or perhaps having lived through the sudden deaths of two husbands, her soul was crushed. It would have been no surprise to learn that she was lonely or worried or uncertain of her circumstances, or maybe she suffered from depression, a state of mind not commonly diagnosed in those days. But whatever embittered Grandma, it gradually pushed us out of her embrace.

CHAPTER 6

Building Blocks of a Strong Start

Start children off on the way they should go,
and even when they are old they will not turn from it.

—Proverbs 22:6

Before leaving for school each day, my older brother Vincent and I shared the duties of taking care of the livestock. We awoke early each morning just as the sun was breaking through the darkness of night. The cool, crisp morning air quickened our senses. The goats and the pigs assembled themselves expectantly as they waited for Vincent to pour the morning feed into each of their trestles. Vincent was also required to clean out the pigs' living quarters each day. He dreaded this task but knew it had to be done.

My duties included feeding the chickens and turkeys and gathering eggs. As I sprinkled their food on the ground, they squawked and fought each other for their portions. I laughed at their antics as the dominant fowl bullied the others for extra feed.

Even my younger siblings understood from an early age the importance of pitching in. In fact, they were eager to help, so they often tried to mimic Vincent and me as we went about carrying out our daily responsibilities. However, I knew that until they were old enough to understand the entire task, they would only make a mess and with them, chore time with the animals would more than likely turn to playtime. My daily routine with the chickens and turkeys continued until I assumed more of the household chores. By then, my younger brothers and sisters stepped in to feed the animals. As their "mini-mom," I focused my spare time in preparing my brothers and sisters for school by teaching them some basic words and simple math.

Historically, Barbadians are known to have one of the highest literacy rates in the world. As I was in a country that was under British rule, I was educated through one of the best school systems available. The school system was divided into primary schools, secondary schools and tertiary levels. Our small local primary school was located in walking distance from our home.

By age four, I was taught the basics of the alphabet, how to write our names, to read simple words and to do basic math. We also had playtime at school, which I really enjoyed. We sang and played simple games outside in the yard. At snack time, the teacher was so kind to provide small homemade *bakes* which she shared with all of her students. The fried bakes were made from a mixture of flour, baking powder, butter, cinnamon/nutmeg spice and sweetened with cane sugar. On Fridays, if we had been well-behaved all week, special treats like coconut bread and tamarind balls would also be shared.

Before we left for school in the morning, Mommy made sure we ate something. I liked the times I would have bread spread with a layer of thick sweet milk. Mommy ensured our uniforms were pristine and that we left home early enough to arrive to school on time. My school building consisted of a large wood frame with windows that had wooden shutters. Each horizontal panel, when opened, allowed the warmth of sunlight to cascade throughout the classroom. On days when it was very hot, the shutters would serve as guardians of light as they were not opened widely, but just enough to allow a cross breeze to flow through and cool down the room. Trees and beautiful greenery surrounded the school. I enjoyed looking at the flowers that bloomed in an intertwined profusion of magenta, burnt orange, deep green, red and golden yellow. Sometimes, as I approached the schoolyard, I imagined I was strolling through a lush impressionistic landscape painting.

During those days, the locally-trained teachers were skilled professionals who provided us with a proper education. They were generally very nice, but they did not tolerate any foolishness, and they did not hesitate to follow island tradition and punish the students when they did not listen or behave. The schoolmistress's preferred instrument of punishment was a ruler. Children who misbehaved or came to school late received a rap across their knuckles with the ruler. This act of discipline demonstrated her authority over any who tempted fate by arriving after the clanging morning school bell had quieted.

The headmistress required all students to take their seats on arrival. One of the students checked attendance prior to the recording of the previous day's homework assignments. Knowing that a knuckle-rapping awaited the slothful student, I always made sure to have my work ready to pass forward for collection each day. Next, we stood and sang with one voice the British anthem, "God Save the Queen," Barbados's patriotic song in those days. I enjoyed singing this song and always felt proud of my island, which at that time was under British rule.

As primary school continued to age eleven, I then enjoyed learning about Barbados' geography. I especially was thrilled as the teacher often chose me to assist her with passing out things like graded papers or poems to the other children. Even in school, leadership skills were reinforced and embedded deep into my soul. I always took care to greet each student properly with a smile as I presented him or her with the day's work. It was an opportunity to interact with my friends outside of recess.

In primary school, I learned a greater depth of reading, writing and math. I enjoyed challenging math formulas and would always remember their foundation when my teachers taught us math by using songs. Sometimes the songs were based on nursery rhymes, and they helped us memorize our multiplication tables in preparation for surprise quizzes. The teachers would ask us to stand up and recite our times tables. Because I hoped to be prepared, I often practiced while walking home from school with my older brother Vincent. We memorized our schoolwork together. The beautiful melodic sounds characteristic of the Barbados accent enhanced the rhythm, "two twos are four, four fours are eight," and so on. With Vincent's help, I learned my multiplication tables well ahead of the other students. By age eleven, everyone who successfully completed the primary level "graduated" and moved forward to the secondary level.

My last two years of school focused on more difficult subjects such as history, science and advanced math. I loved math. I liked adding up my grocery bill in my head while shopping simply because I enjoyed working with numbers. (Plus, it never hurts to double check the salesclerk!) We did not have individual textbooks, so the teacher explained the lesson, read from the book and then wrote examples on the blackboard for students to review. Because Barbados was a British Commonwealth colony, we were taught the "proper way" to speak English. For example, we called a *zero* a *naught* and an *apartment* a *flat*. We were proud to learn the Queen's English.

We also studied poetry and shared our poems with the class. I always recited poems from memory rather than reading them. I liked to stand tall and look straight into the eyes of my fellow classmates as I shared. One of my favorite poems by William Wordsworth is titled "Lucy Gray." I liked this poem because it tells a story of a young girl named Lucy and her caring parents. When Lucy was lost in the snow, her parents looked everywhere in the snowy wilderness hoping to find her. Even though her footprints led them to a bridge where it appears she has fallen, the parents are able to comfort one another that God is in control. I kept the Lucy Gray poem secretly in my childish heart for years. When I travel down memory lane, I often recite the poem to family just for the pure fun of it.

At the end of the school day, I would hurry home to help Mommy prepare the evening meal for the family. In those days, there were no gas or electric stoves as we know them today. Daddy would chop and store wood which was then burned in our cook stove. The cook stove was large and made of cast iron. It was located outside, behind the house. With the heat in the tropics, it was better to keep any additional heat outside. As our stove could burn either wood or coal, my brother Vincent would go to the backyard to gather the coal or the wood to start the fire each evening.

Once gathered, Vincent placed the wood in the large hole in the center of the stove. When the flames reached a suitable level, he would place a large, water-filled metal canister on top the stove to boil. When it had percolated to the required temperature, Mommy or I would begin to cook. Traditionally, we ate peas and rice on Sundays. It was prepared with fresh herbs and seasoning, scallions, and salted beef or pig tail to add a rich flavor to the rice before adding in the peas. To soften the peas and to remove any pebbles, the peas had to be soaked from the night before. I looked forward to Sunday lunch when pork or chicken stew was prepared as a tasty feast for the family. A meal with beef was a special dish in those days, reserved for a special treat.

Each night before eating, it was our family ritual to first gather to pray and to share with each other what had happened during our day. Then, finally, with joy and thanksgiving, we ate dinner.

I always found the act of cooking for my loved ones to be rewarding because it allowed me a daily opportunity to express my love for my family in a tangible way. Mommy, too, loved to cook, whether it was for our everyday, at-the-table meals or for special picnics we sometimes enjoyed in the backyard. It always seemed to me that she could prepare a veritable feast from even the simplest of local meats, vegetables, fresh herbs and seasonings. She used the ingredients she had in combinations that would surely challenge the skills of any top chef. I am certain that many of the tasty meals she created back before her aliments kicked in would be popular today if collected in a cookbook. My mother, however, did not work from a cookbook so I made a special effort to remember everything she taught me when preparing the Sunday meal.

Sometimes Mommy and I would have fun teasing each other while we cooked. "Margaret, please wash and cut up the sweet potato." "Mommy, where is the pot for the sweet potato?" "Sweetie, it's on dah table." "I don't see it, Mommy." "Cheese-on-bread! It is right behind you!" "Yes, I see it now, Mommy." "Oh, I'm glad a black bird did not come and pick out your eyes!" Then her voice would ring out with laughter and soon I was joining in. I enjoyed the special cooking times with my mother. She taught me all the family cooking secrets. Mommy might have served the simplest of meals, but knowing she had prepared them with love for us children made them the tastiest meals on earth to me.

During the week, dinner at home often consisted of "dry-food" (slices of boiled sweet potato, English potatoes, breadfruit, carrots, plaintain, yams and dumplings served with a salted cod fish gravy, or corned beef or salted herring gravy); split pea soup with chicken backs; boiled and mashed breadfruit with stewed down salt fish gravy; or the Barbadian national dish corn meal Cou Cou served with steamed flying fish. When preparing flying fish, I would often envision how these fish would make self-propelling leaps from the water and glide through the air before returning to the sea. I think flying fish are interesting and delicious fried or stewed. They are found in the warm waters surrounding Barbados, and are about 9 inches long. Often likened to a herring, flying fish have fins that to me look like wings.

Before I could sit down to partake of whatever was on our menu each evening, I would prepare a plate for mommy. Daddy wouldn't arrive home till later in the evening, but out of respect I would prepare his plate next and set it aside. Then I served the children. By this time they had endured a long day and were ready for dinner. Then it was finally my turn to sit down to eat. Even though we had small portions, it was enough.

One evening as I sat eating my meal, I remembered one particular day when my brother and I were walking through the chattel properties on our way home from school. I recalled noticing how the houses, although in similar grey and brown color tones, each expressed the residents' unique personalities. The chattel homes sat on coral block foundations and were primarily constructed from very dry, pre-cut timber imported from either the United States or South America. This was a perfect choice of wood for building homes in the tropics. Most of the chattel houses were almost exactly the same size and shape — perfectly square and topped with a gable roof design with embedded grooves which allow rain from the frequent tropical showers to easily roll off. The architecture was simple, and it was a mobile home concept that allowed owners to add on to the house as their income improved or even to dismantle the building and move it to another location.

During the late afternoon, a residue of the day's heat seemed to linger. On this particular day, I was thinking about how I could cool off when suddenly Vincent and I heard a loud explosion, as if a mountain had collapsed and fallen into the sea. I quickly raised my trembling hands to block the blazing sun from my eyes so that I could focus my sight in the direction from which the frightening noise had come.

Out to sea, a large object burned on the water. Flames rose upward, reaching high into the sky which rapidly filled with gunpowder-colored clouds. Frantically searching for an explanation, I spotted a large, grey ship: it was the *Cornwallis*. The accomplished goal of a mighty warrior boat had apparently been to destroy it with a torpedo.

Though it was a startling tragedy, my brother's immediate instinct was for us to race to the shoreline on the chance that some of the food the ship would have delivered would float ashore. Many quickly moving townspeople, including Vincent and me, were able to rescue non-perishable items that washed onto the beach.

Vincent, only 18 months older than I, exuded a level of authority that I still admire today. The authoritative presence he had was only strengthened by the fact that at a very young age he was prescribed to wear glasses. The spectacles made him appear much older than his years and lent him a strong, authoritative manner. As an older brother, he really lived up to his "look of authority."

Over the years our conversations spanned topics as diverse as politics, economics and more. He was intelligent, yes, but also sometimes a little bit stubborn — even when his view was incorrect. Although I didn't always agree with him, I so admired this strong trait that I seldom argued with his conclusions. With his substantial height, his broad shoulders, dark hair and brown eyes, Vincent presented the air of an imperturbable leader. He walked through life with upheld head, undaunted by potential dangers yet to be faced. His protectiveness toward me often discouraged his male friends from talking with me when they came to our home to visit. He made it clear to his "boys" that I was *his* little sister: "She's off limits," he told them. His friends could say hello to me, but then must back off. I treasured Vincent's protectiveness. It made me feel very safe whenever I wandered on my own along the slender roadways of the island.

Vincent's protection extended into my school life. I recall an incident that happened when I was about twelve years old. I arrived home from school one afternoon in tears. Vincent insisted on knowing what had upset me. Through my tears, I told him how some of the older girls at school were teasing me. As I walked home, they walked behind me and jarred me, saying, "Margaret at the cottage gate, eating dumplings off she plate. When she finished, lick she plate. Two, four, six, eight." This incident truly upset Vincent. He told me to stop crying and comforted me, saying that he would take care of everything and for me not to worry.

The next afternoon, I was walking home from school when the same group of girls followed me and began their usual teasing ritual. However, on this day, Vincent arrived on the scene, too. He jumped off his bicycle and placing himself between them and me, he scolded the girls, saying, "Listen here! You like to run your mouth about foolishness! You bother my sister again and I will give you a backhand lash!"

When they heard the word *lash*, the girls ran away. We could see in these girls' eyes that they were truly frightened by Vincent, who seemed especially tall and imposing that particular afternoon. He had delivered a serious warning to my tormentors, and they knew that he meant business — his tone of voice left them in no doubt that he would follow through. Not surprisingly, this incident put an end to my problems with these girls.

CHAPTER 7

Free at Last

*The LORD himself goes before you
and will be with you;
he will never leave you nor forsake you.
Do not be afraid; do not be discouraged.*

—Deuteronomy 31:8

T he youth of my era were encouraged to enroll in higher education. After receiving my School Leaving Certificate (similar to
the American diploma), at age 14, I decided I wanted to go on to university having attended the Carrington Village School. So as I blos-
somed into a young lady, I looked for opportunities that could help
pay for university. I came across an application for the Miss Barbados
beauty contest. The cash prize I would receive if I won would provide
me the opportunity to attend university. I had begun to appreciate my
attractive features and my shapely figure, inherited from my diverse
family lineage, and my confidence grew. I became brave enough, at
age 15, to enter the beauty contest in which I would compete with
nine other contestants.

The contestants were judged on personality, evening wear and
swimwear. I felt very secure as the judges asked their questions during
the personality portion of the competition. With solid proclamation
and clear projection, I answered each question without hesitation.
Everything was going well, and then came the swimwear portion of
the competition. I was wearing a beautiful pink one-piece swimsuit

with a matching, detachable ruffled skirt. The waistband of the skirt was secured with a button located at the back of the garment. During the swimwear presentation, the contestants were given an opportunity to describe their choice of costume. While describing to the judges the details of the detachable ruffle, I proceeded to demonstrate the versatility of the design. But due to the small size of the buttonhole, I was unable to properly unbutton the ruffle from the suit. This unfortunate fumble caused me to place third in the overall pageant. Even though third place was a very respectable position, I was still disappointed. University was not to be. Many of my friends did go on to university and then achieved great careers. In my case, due to a lack of funds, I was not able to pursue my own dreams of a higher education.

One evening, I sat on the edge of the bed, looking at my graduation School Leaving Certificate I held in my hand, and began to plot a new course. I told myself that if I wanted to be self-supportive, I would need to find a part-time job. As part of my plan, I would continue to help Mommy, but I would also train my sisters to do the same. I truly believed that once I was in a work environment, other opportunities for personal improvement and progress would find their way into my life. I was nervous about my plan, but excited, too. I was finally taking charge of my destiny. But there was no one with whom to share my new strategy. I was certain my parents would disapprove, and my father might not even take me seriously — after all, I was known in the family to be the mini-mommy. I decided to keep my ambitious ideas about my future a secret from everyone, even my brother, Vincent, with whom I was very close. As much as he loved me, he was still a traditional Bajan man and he would not understand. Besides, his head was full of the plans he was making for his own future.

When Vincent turned eighteen, he had decided to live in England. I remember the pain I felt when I realized he would be leaving. He had been my rock and protector for all the years I grew up. Now he would be far away. We had played together as children and were very close. I did not want him to leave. Yet I knew that this was his chance to move on and become the man he envisioned himself to someday be, and I was so proud of him.

Vincent packed his personal items: a few vest shirts, his dark tie, a navy suit and his black shoes. Mommy placed a Bible in his suitcase, to remind him of his strong foundation of faith learned at home. The money he had saved from working at a local store was just enough to pay for a one-way boat ticket and expenses for a month. I was concerned about how he would survive on his own: we had no friends or family in England at that time. Vincent assured me that he would be all right and that, once he was settled, he would write and give me his new address and tell me all about England.

I will never forget the day he left. It was time to pack Vincent's suitcase and personal items into the neighbor's truck. Daddy was not there to see Vincent off, as he had to work that night. As the rest of the family stood by the waiting vehicle, Vincent hugged and kissed each of us. When it was Mommy's turn, she said, "Vincent, you have made me so proud. You stepped in whenever I needed you and never complained once." She reached into the pocket of her apron. In her hand was a well-preserved but tarnished change purse. She opened it to reveal a roll of English currency. Reaching her fingertips inside, she grasped the currency and removed it all. "Here is a little something I have been saving." She pressed the money into Vincent's hand and told him, "God be with you." Tears streaming down her face, she next placed a strand of rosary beads around his neck and embraced him.

The goodbyes were over and it was truly time to leave. I went with Vincent to catch his ship. The sun had settled and the air was quiet as we drove in contemplative silence to the docks. Once there, we stood in the stillness of the evening, preternaturally aware of the ramp that led up to the deck of Vincent's boat and, ultimately, to his departure from our daily lives. Finally, I turned to my brother. Though I felt like crying, I said, "Have fun, Vincent," adding a tremulous smile for good measure. He hugged me again and then turned to walk onto the boat. I could bear it no more. Turning toward the car, I broke down in a flowing river of tears. In that moment it seemed that every moment of fun and laughter Vincent and I had ever shared ran through my mind.

The sound of the ship's horn brought me back to present day and confirmed that Vincent was indeed on his way. For now, there would be no turning back. Slowly the ship sailed in the warmth of the sky-blue Barbadian sea, disappearing somewhere into the horizon. Vincent, my big brother, who had for so long watched over me, was gone from my life, leaving a gap such as I had never experienced. For the first week or so, I stumbled through my days, missing his company more than I had ever imagined I could miss anyone. We exchanged letters, of course, but it was several years before we spoke again, due to the expense of phone calls in those days. Nevertheless, distance had no power over the cherished memories we shared. On the contrary, with Vincent in mind, I was emotionally empowered to walk in his footsteps as the eldest of the children living at home.

My mother would say, "Margaret, you are gracefully transitioning from teenager to young adult." With her vote of confidence, I planned that the next time I went with Daddy to Bridgetown I'd beg him profusely to allow me to find employment

During the spirited events of our next family shopping trip to the vendor market, I was given a job reference for a store clerk position in the city of Bridgetown by a friend of the family. Even then I realized God works in mysterious ways. I turned to Daddy for approval. After deep consideration, he agreed. "Margaret, I think that you are old enough, and have the right caliber of education and home training to go to work." Beside myself with enthusiasm, I smiled as deep and wide as the Atlantic ocean.

Months later, I was employed as a store clerk then was promoted to supervisor. While working in this occupation I took classes in shorthand, typewriting and bookkeeping. Thank God for my drive to learn as it was all uphill from this day job. One day when I took a lunch break from work, I found myself chatting with a young lady also eating lunch at the restaurant.

"Oh, that flying fish sandwich looks so good," I said.

"Thank you, your cheese cutter doesn't look too bad, either," she said.

We both smiled.

"My name is Kathy. What is yours?"

"It's Margaret. I work near this restaurant and I take classes in the evening, so I'm sure we'll run into each other again. Enjoy your lunch."

"Well, unfortunately, I am leaving my company for a position at another company offering a higher salary, but it's located in St. John, so I only have three weeks to run into you before moving on. Do you mind if I ask what you do?"

When I told her, she then inquired about the classes I was taking. She said, "Perfect!"

"What do you mean?" I asked.

"I am an accountant and my current company is looking for someone to replace me. I am happy to pass on your information as a referral, if you are interested."

"Yes, thank you!" I was overjoyed as an accounting position would mean a title and a double salary promotion. We exchanged contact information. "Good luck in your new position Kathy." We hugged.

"It was really wonderful meeting you, Margaret," Kathy said. "I will set up an interview for you in a week. So I'll see you then."

Smiling from ear to ear, I waved goodbye. I rejoiced internally and started to think about the God my Mommy told us about and how He appeared to be really working on my behalf. I applied for the position and was hired immediately.

These jobs allowed me to meet new people, like Heinz who worked in the department next to mine. He took a liking to me and would take me out on dates. This transition to adulthood was just what I needed to spread my wings.

Because I was away during the day, I was less accessible to Daddy when he would come home from work in the late afternoon, having stopped to have a drink or two. Arriving home after Daddy, I often found him resting. Although it appeared that Daddy must have grown to accept me as an adult during my working years, he continued to physically trouble me.

CHAPTER 8

Love Lifted Me

For God so loved the world
that he gave his one and only son
that whoever believes in him shall not perish
but have eternal life.

—John 3:16

My 21st birthday was a landmark season in my life. I took the time to sit and reflect on my life's current landscape and how far I'd come. Despite my ongoing mental and emotional scars that I hoped would have the chance to heal, if they ever healed at all — I still had my health, and I worked for a prestigious and well-known accountant on the island. I was reaching a point of independence from all my previous responsibilities at home. Yet, in spite of all I had achieved, I felt emptiness. A sick, misled jealousy sometimes unleashed an indefinite dread I could neither identify nor escape. It all started when I got ill. I learned that it was a result of my loving yet unconscionable father's misbehavings outside of the family. He was having an affair with a young lady who worked at the prison. So when I eventually turned 21, I went with my friends to have a good time away from it all. I got regretfully drunk. It was so bad that I decided it was the first and last time I'd lose my sobriety.

In the 1950s, Barbadians were talking about the buzz around the great preacher Billy Graham's visit to Barbados from the United States. Pastor Graham would hold a two-day crusade and the entire island was immensely enthusiastic about it. My coworker Vanessa and I talked about how Barbados had never experienced a visit from such a famous leader in the Christian faith. We had both heard of his work and ministry in other countries and how it was building the faith of the people. We were thrilled he had chosen to visit our island.

"Margaret, are you available to attend the Billy Graham Crusade tomorrow? It's the first night and I would be so happy if you'd go with me?" Vanessa asked.

"Heinz asked me last week if I'd go out for dinner with him. In all honesty, things do not look to be working out between he and I, so I would much rather go with you, Vanessa."

"Margaret, sorry to hear that. I hope you can work things out with Heinz. Maybe he can join us? I think he'll enjoy it. But we would have to get there early as I hear all the crusades are packed with thousands of attendees."

"Vanessa, this crusade is unfamiliar to me. I was raised as a devoted Roman Catholic. I didn't at all mind going to mass with Mommy when I was a child. Maybe it's the right time to give church another try."

The crusade was held at the local racetrack, the largest venue in the Christ Church parish. The racetrack, usually host only to special sporting events and large concerts, had been beautifully transformed to an outdoor sanctuary for the crusade. As Heinz was not interested in attending the crusade, Vanessa and I left work early so that we could get good seats. When we arrived, it seemed that thousands of others — many of them other curious Roman Catholics — had the same idea! The people were noisy and excited, and the air was filled with equal parts anticipation and curiosity. Vanessa and I pressed through the staggering crowd and after a short time found two seats together. We eagerly got settled.

Now, as the stadium spotlights focused in tightly on the erected stage, a glorious song filled the atmosphere and gave me goose bumps. The music was gentle and harmonious. Even with the tropical warmth that rolled across the seats and blew my hair into my eyes, I still felt an attention awakening chill. As the song faded away, the service opened with a word of prayer. Then came the moment everyone had been so anxiously awaiting, the introduction of the guest preacher, Dr. Billy Graham.

Tall in stature, Billy Graham walked to the podium amidst a thunderous cheer of welcome. His dark grey suit, offset by a white collared shirt, resembled the customary garb worn by every other Christian missionary or pastor I'd ever seen, but there was something indefinably different about him. Everyone sensed it, and many — Protestants, Roman Catholic and the non-affiliated alike — stood to welcome this man whom they apparently considered a representative from God.

Dr. Graham, standing in front of the lectern, stood there for a moment and with a pensive look on his face, seemed to scan the audience as if he were looking for someone specific. In that moment, I could almost believe that he was searching for me alone. I suspect many others felt the same. And then he spoke. His deep tones, clear and confident, immediately flooded the large venue and bellowed with a force like a thunderstorm. He taught that evening as one with authority, reading scriptures from the Holy Bible, never compromising the word of the Lord. I was enthralled!

At the end of the night, to the beautiful hymn "Just as I Am" softly being sung in the background, Dr. Billy Graham further shared the love of God by inviting all to have a personal relationship with God's son, Jesus. He beckoned those in the stadium to come to the altar for prayer. He welcomed all who would come. I felt such a sincerity of spirit when in that moment prayers went out as people were accepting Jesus into their hearts. Jesus was introduced as a friend who will stick closer than a brother. We were compelled, no matter our circumstance or place in life, to come to Jesus. He taught that Jesus died for our sins so that we can live forgiven lives. A massive amount of people throughout the venue joined Dr. Graham at the altar and came to Jesus.

I recognized a tugging in my own heart and felt an increasing desire to give my life to Jesus. I was hesitant and afraid. I had never experienced such an overwhelming level of emotion and excitement, feeling of forgiveness and promise of hope. Next to me, my friend Vanessa, a Christian, was praying aloud that God would work a miracle in me. I wanted to step forward, but there were questions in my mind about the God that Billy Graham spoke of: could Jesus really love me, with all my guilt and shame? Was I really worthy of such unconditional love?

The choir continued to sing, and the words of "Just as I Am" seeped into my soul. I started to sing the words. Suddenly I found myself standing and walking forward, making my way to the altar, to make the acquaintance of Jesus from a personal perspective. Now, whenever I hear "Just As I am," it reminds me of the night I gave my heart to the Lord. As I walked to the altar, my heart pounded and my hands shook. I walked with bowed head and anxiously prayed, "Lord, I am a sinner. I ask you to take away all the pain and hurt within me. I know that you love and forgive me, Lord. I believe that your Son, Jesus, was crucified died and was buried and has risen and lives forevermore at the right hand of God our Father. He arose, and I accept Him within my heart. I am free. In Jesus' name. Amen."

That night, I knew the Lord forgave me of my sins and came into my heart. Such a revelation of being loved by God, the creator of everything, was comforting and knowing that God's spirit will be with me even until the end of the earth was empowering. That night I experienced the presence of almighty God. All the burdens of my past and all that Daddy had done to me for years were laid at the feet of Jesus. I would no longer carry the burden. The Lord set free my bottled-up shame and gave me the ability to forgive my father. Peace of mind and hope for the future became my balm, my therapy, and the joy of the Lord became my medicine.

The next night, my two sisters, Paris and Jennifer, went with me to hear Billy Graham speak, and they also gave their hearts to the Lord. We hugged each other and cried together, joyfully relinquishing our past and understanding that, no matter what trials we had experienced in our lives, this was the turning point. My sisters and I found a local church and were baptized as soon as possible. As a start of our Christian spiritual journey, baptism expressed an outward sign of an inward change. As I was submerged in the warm, calm ocean waters that surrounded our beautiful island, I sensed my Savior's presence. I felt lighter as I was lifted out of the water, as though the weight of this world was raised from my shoulders. Once I was wrapped with a white towel, it felt as if a blanket of peacefulness had surrounded my newfound hope. I felt revived and renewed! As part of my new normalcy, I placed my trust in His model of healing, forgiveness and in the love of God, my neighbor and myself.

One night after service, I came home totally confident in God but completely exhausted. I darted straight for my room as if I were an arrow and my bed the bullseye. I kicked off my shoes and outer garments and rapidly pulled on my cotton, lace-trimmed, pure white nightgown. In no time I was in a deep sleep. Then what seemed like shortly after, I was slowly awoken out of a bottomless slumber by an endearing deep voice that talked about wanting to make me happy.

It was Daddy. His lips kissed my neck and moved slowly to once again taste the juice of my natural melons. But this was not going to happen. When I came to myself, I sat up in my bed and in the resolution of my newly-found faith in God, I looked Daddy straight in his eyes and unwaveringly said, "Daddy I cannot do this anymore. I am saved now!"

Without hesitation or an uttered word, Daddy got up and left my bedroom. Immediately I began to pray. I cried myself to sleep, all the while thanking Jesus for strength from His comforting Holy Spirit to put an end to Daddy's conditioned emotional and physical abuse. That night was a true victory over evil. Daddy never troubled me again.

***

The following months were a great time in our lives. My sisters and I spent Wednesday evenings at Bible study, Thursdays at choir rehearsal and Fridays with the youth organization. We were all very happy to be volunteering our time in the local protestant church. Later that year, I was elected by vote to the office of young people's president for Youth For Christ. I was overjoyed! The main responsibility of the role was to hold weekly meetings with the teenagers and those up to age 23 in the church, and explain to them the love and kindness of Jesus. I and my sisters who helped me used many methods to get this message across, such as when we organized a musical concert at church with Paris, Jennifer and I singing as a trio, along with our church choir.

Our church congregation grew and became even stronger spiritually, as more and more youth continued to embrace scripture teachings. Many young people were saved through the efforts of youth-specific meetings and events. But my sisters and I knew that we were only God's messengers and that He was using us for His own purposes. He was and always would be in ultimate control, and that was fine with us. We were happy to do His work in whatever miraculous fashion He chose.

One evening during my third youth revival service, a young man, who happened to look very familiar to me, stepped forward to commit his life to Christ. At the time, I did not make any particular fuss about him, but I did notice that he was tall, very slim in stature with black wavy hair, a tan complexion and a round, heart-shaped face. He wore a basic vest shirt with white pants and white shoes. Later, I realized how much I *had* noticed about him — right down to his shoes. I also took note that when he returned to his seat from the altar, he kept his head down for the rest of the evening. He came back again to the next night's service and sat at the back of the church, as he had previously done. This time, at the end of the night's evening, a few of the members of the youth group and I approached him to introduce ourselves.

"Hi, my name is Margaret. Did you enjoy Pastor's message tonight?"

"Yes."

"Do you live nearby? You look so familiar."

"Not too far."

"And your name?" I inquired, like a reporter conducting an interview.

"Benton Matias. But my friends call me Ben," he added with a smile, as if he knew me.

"Benton, nice to meet you," was my cordial response. "I am the president of the young people's organization, Youth for Christ. We meet once a week on Fridays. Maybe you would like to join us?"

"That sounds good."

"Hope to see you there."

At that moment, he reached out to shake my hand. His hand, warm and smooth — unusually so for a man his age — was an indication that he did not spend much time working in the Barbados sugarcane fields. Perhaps he spent his time reading to become more educated, as I had done, I thought. I chose that moment to look him in the eye. In that moment I sensed a loneliness. I had no idea what had caused his sadness, but I felt compelled to befriend him.

From that moment on, the youth committee members encouraged Benton's church attendance. During the next few months, Benton seemed very acclimated to the things of God as if he'd attended a church before ours. He became very active in our congregation, right alongside the youth members. He attended the youth group meetings, and he soon joined various church committees that helped those in need. Whatever loneliness he may have felt, it never seemed to hold him back from interacting with others. He was charismatic, and the teenagers — as well as many of their parents — were captivated by the sound of his voice, his friendly demeanor, as well as his confident posture. Soon he was being asked to speak at various gatherings. I later found out that Benton's mother passed when he was just 5 years old, his father moved out of the country to England and started another family, and that he was being raised by a missionary family.

When Benton spoke before a crowd, he tended to wave his arms as though he were conducting an orchestra. And somehow, each person in his audience was always right with him, like finely tuned symphonic instruments. Instinctively, Benton could reach those who were lonely and discouraged, and he was not afraid to challenge big, tough men who would often later humble themselves before Christ.

Inevitably, I was drawn to Benton's spirit. Seeing so many young people coming to the Lord after hearing him preach, I felt this man was someone I could follow in the ministry. The pastor was so impressed with Benton's work in ministry that he appointed him as the Youth For Christ youth pastor. With this title, Benton seemed to have found his true calling. As he grew in knowledge by studying the Bible, he began traveling to different parishes to share the love of God. Many teens throughout the island were saved from their reckless sinful ways under his ministry. As Benton grew in popularity among the many churches on the island, the pastor decided Benton's ministry would be even more effective if Paris, Jennifer and I joined him as the musical inspiration for his services. We eagerly agreed. We sang as Benton held each congregation captive with his powerful teachings from the Bible. Our musical/preaching combination was a great success. Many people were transformed and joined the churches we visited throughout the island.

On Saturdays, Benton would pick us up in his dusty blue Austin. We knew he had arrived when we heard the low rumbling of his car outside. Benton's car was a bit old, but it was big enough to take us all where we needed to go. As we raced through the island's narrow streets, going quickly from one church to the next, the car's only air conditioning was the fresh air that flowed from window to window cooling our sweaty brows with warm cross-ventilation. Before starting our journeys, we always took time to pray for the work we would do with those who would hear us that day. We prepared ourselves to pray with them so as to strengthen their faith in God. Benton was always enthusiastic about sharing the word of God.

One day on our way home, it was just the two of us — Paris and Jennifer could not make it that day — so we exchanged observations, as we always did, chatting about all the good that God was working in our lives. During our visits to the different churches, our throats would get dry as we talked about the many obstacles we often dealt with, such as arranging transportation. On this one occasion, Benton suddenly turned to look straight at me. As our eyes locked, I remembered our first meeting at the revival service the year before.

"Margaret, I'm falling in love with you."

I stared at him, speechless. Love? My concept of a male's love was quite mixed at the time. How did Benton define love? Was it one dimensional, only a path to a sexual experience? Or was his an emotionally-connected love like Jesus had for humanity when he lived and died for us? I knew too little about men and their ways; after all, so far, I'd only had a distorted example. So many questions were racing through my mind that, for a long moment, I only stared back at Benton, not speaking at all.

Finally, regaining my composure, I stammered out that I would have to pray about it.

Soon thereafter, Benton dropped me off at home and I ran inside to be alone with my thoughts and pray about what Benton said.

***

A few days later, as was his custom, he came to pick me up from work. Benton usually looked quite neat and clean. But on this day, the shoes he was wearing looked shabby, as if he had worn them during some kind of heavy labor. I noticed that the sole of his left shoe was falling off. I sensed that something more was going on and I felt sympathy for him. In that moment, with sudden clarity I knew that when Benton was "broken," I could be emotionally there for him. At the time, I did not have foresight as to the level of responsibility a relationship with Benton would demand.

One afternoon, Benton told me that he had spent the day at the church. All day he was fasting and praying, seeking God's guidance for the next steps in his life. He said that during this time God had revealed to him that he should marry me.

I was stunned. I had only recently realized that I might care for him, and here he was already talking about marriage. Was my heart ready for all of this? I needed to know for myself if marriage to Benton was part of God's plan for my life.

We sat in Benton's car and talked more about his experience that day. At last he told me that while at church, he had opened his Bible and was led to the scripture Matthew 1:20: "…Joseph son of David, do not be afraid to take Mary home as your wife…."

"I don't know," I said. "This is all very sudden." My heart was pounding, grasping that unconsciously I had longed to hear those words. And now, hearing that he spent time praying and that he was led to a scripture reference—I was quite overwhelmed as he was hitting all the right chords of my heart. Stunned, I said, "Benton, are you kidding me? What will my parents think?"

"Margaret, I spoke with your father and he said it was ok."

"You did? Really?" I then thought, *I cannot guarantee that all Benton is saying is strictly true.* Now I had to decide if what Benton wanted was also right for me. Rather than rush into anything serious, I suggested that we take it slow by telling our friends that we were officially courting. I could see fear and disappointment on Benton's face. He had indirectly asked me to marry him, but I needed more time to talk to my parents directly and do some heavy praying to God to confirm if this was the man for me. I later found out that he had a ring in his pocket that he wanted to give to me.

After a couple of weeks, I was confused when I did not get what I would consider a clear answer to my prayers, but since Benton was so certain that his answer came from God, I was reluctant to ignore his proposal for much longer. Benton was a spiritual man. I should trust him, I thought. Besides, the Bible says a man that finds a wife finds a good thing. So I agreed to marry Benton once we both finished Bible college.

***

We planned an engagement announcement party for June 30, 1961, and invited all our new friends from various churches and people from our jobs. More than fifty people attended our dinner party, which we held at the home of one of the church's very good members. Special dishes and pastries had been prepared for the event. I still remember the wonderful joy I experienced that day because Benton made me feel like the queen of the island. That day, there was no discussion about ministry or upcoming events. I became the center of his attention for all to see and celebrate. Many of the single women had a spark of admiration in their eyes. I held hands with Benton as our guests departed, graciously smiling and thanking each and every person for attending. After waving goodbye to the last guest, Benton and I remained outside on the veranda, and he held me in his arms. It was one of the high points in my life.

"Blossom," Benton said, using the nickname he had given me after we became engaged, "look up into the sky. You see all those stars? One day I will go and gather them for you. Your life will shine so bright because you decided to be with me. Anything you want, I will give to you. If you want the moon, I will give that to you. I will love you and only you. Thank you, Blossom, for giving me this chance."

His words were beautiful, and the moment was truly momentous. But as he continued to whisper sweet words to me, I could not say why my mind was suddenly flooded with a small pang of alarm as I unexpectedly recalled a phrase my mother often repeated: "Wha' sweet in goat mouth does burn in his bam bam." I had learned that what may seem sweet and good at one moment can have painful consequences later. I should have listened to that small frisson of alarm that ran through me, but the night was so beautiful, and I felt beautiful too, so I then cherished Benton.

CHAPTER 9

Appearance of Love

But among you there must not be even a hint of sexual immorality,
or of any kind of impurity, or greed,
because these are improper for God's holy people.

—Ephesians 5:3

Soon after our engagement party, Benton left for the island of Jamaica. He had been accepted into the Jamaica Theological Seminary, located in the heart of Kingston. This university primarily serves Jamaicans and Caribbeans. I did not want him to go away, we were only just engaged, and now he was leaving. Benton told me he had fasted and prayed to be accepted. I tried to accept that if this was what God had for our lives, then it would work out.

Prior to this, Benton had started a business selling fabric to people in the neighborhood. It was a great business for Benton since he was already traveling around the island preaching. Many people to whom he ministered also felt inclined to buy his merchandise. Ultimately, he did very well with the business.

When Benton went away to school, the plan was that I would collect the money from his customers. I had a full-time job and was attending Bible college so I could only work on Saturdays, when I was not busy with church duties. While he was gone, I had the use of his Austin, which was very handy, especially on the weekends when I went out to collect the money. However, after a few weeks I had to give up because Benton's customers would not acknowledge me as the "real owner" of his business and would not pay me.

Benton did not communicate with me much while he was away at college. I assumed he was busy studying and tried not to be concerned. In the one letter Benton sent, he shared that in the midst of studying he would find time to pray and fast. I was so proud to learn he was using his time to get closer to God that I resolved not to be anxious when I didn't hear from him. This situation went on for about a year. To keep myself distracted, I made my job and my responsibilities as youth leader my main areas of focus.

One evening, having returned home after attending a youth service at our church, I received a phone call from Pastor Barret. He was a prominent member and deacon of my church. He asked me to please come by his home immediately because both he and his wife needed to speak with me. I was exhausted and asked if we could get together the next day, but Pastor Barret insisted that it must be that evening. Pastor and Mrs. Barret were very good friends to Benton and me, and they were loved and respected in our church and by everyone who knew them. I also knew that Pastor Barret had stayed in touch with Benton since he'd been gone, and it suddenly came to me that maybe he had news from Benton that he wanted to share with me in person. I told him I would be at his front door as soon as possible. Because it was so late at night, my sister Paris went with me. Pastor Barret's home was a rust and camel colored parsonage that stood out from the adjacent church, due in no small part to the colorful, well-groomed flower beds Mrs. Barret maintained around the front veranda. Paris and I walked up to the house and knocked on the door. Waiting for the Barretts to answer the door, Paris laughingly announced that this had better be good, as she needed to get her beauty sleep.

Just at that moment a tall, dark figure approached us from the back of the home. To my surprise, it was Benton! He approached, smiling at me then greeting me with a passionate kiss. At that moment Paris realized what Pastor Barret's big surprise was all about and excused herself from the presence of us love birds and headed back home. Still dazed and surprised, I could not speak, so I waited for Benton to explain why he was back on the island.

"Blossom, a terrible thing happened at the school. It is a conspiracy."

"A — what?" I responded warily.

Benton looked worried, as if he might be in trouble. My surprise at seeing him back on the island was beginning to subside, and now I was starting to feel a bit bewildered. He showed up in the middle of the night with no warning.

"Blossom," Benton said hastily. "It was not my fault. I was doing my lessons at the school, but they — the people in charge — just did not like me. They felt that I was too broad-minded and outspoken. I tell you, it was a conspiracy!"

He reached out to take my hands, but as I looked into his eyes, they suddenly transported me to a very cold place. I pulled back my hands quickly. "Benton, you are not making sense. What happened at the school? You are not telling me anything."

"You're not listening to me, Margaret!" He raised his voice, as if a louder volume would make me understand his lack of justification. "I tell you, I am innocent! You think I am lying? My own fiancée does not believe me? Who can I trust?"

There was rage in his eyes such as I'd never seen before, and I realized at that moment that I could actually be afraid of Benton under certain circumstances — such as right now. I pulled back to listen to his story. "Just — just tell me what happened," I stammered.

"I was leaving our last class for the day and was talking with one of my fellow students about the previous homework assignment. This was an important assignment that I needed to complete for the final grade. The student, Shelly, offered to let me borrow her notes so that I could study for the test. We went back to her dorm grounds to get the notes, and then I headed back to my dorm. But in the meantime, one of Shelly's classmates saw me on the girls' dorm grounds and told the floor captain that I was there."

"Benton, didn't you know better?"

"Woman, can you just please listen? The authorities accused me of being near the girls' rooms – which is a restricted area and off-limits to the guys. Blossom, this is not true, but they expelled me from the school anyway."

"They — what?!" I cried. "They expelled you from school?"

"Margaret, It's okay," Benton said quickly.

His words echoed in my head and brought with them many questions that I wanted to ask, but at this moment I could not seem to get them out of my mouth. No one else but Pastor and Mrs. Barret, and now Paris and I, knew that Benton was back on the island, much less that he had been expelled from his school during finals. I wondered what people would think when word finally got around about Benton's devastating news and the embarrassment he would now have to contend with for having to finish his schooling in Barbados instead of Jamaica. People would talk and assume only the worst. Whatever their version of the worst might be, the truth of it was standing next to me: Benton was expelled.

Benton worked at convincing me that the incident at the theological seminary was truly a conspiracy and reminded me how much he was still in love with me. Why Benton would be singled out as the subject of anyone's conspiracy, I did not understand. I thought about the importance of trust in any good relationship and I wanted everything to work out, so I finally decided to let it go and give Benton another chance. In the interest of love and trust one for another, I pushed aside my concerns about what might have really happened in Jamaica.

I buried my nose in my own studies at the Bible college in Barbados and I successfully completed a three-year certificate program the college offered. I was totally enthralled with learning. As a result, the college allowed me to study books of the Old and New Testaments in detail. The teachers required us to memorize many verses, and this reminded me a lot of my early school years, which I had enjoyed so much. Knowing these verses by heart came in very handy many times in my life.

We students also had very thought-provoking conversations among ourselves. I incorporated much of what I learned into the weekly lessons I taught to the members of Youth for Christ at my church.

Benton enrolled at the school I was attending, came back to church and we grew spiritually and romantically.

Sometimes Benton would pick me up from work, and we would drive around the countryside, laughing and enjoying each other's company. During these times we'd often stop at the local shop to enjoy a sweet treat together. Benton never made any inappropriate moves. He honored the fact that we were both Christians, and I felt safe with him. As time slipped by, I felt more and more comfortable with Benton and fell more deeply in love with him than ever.

After Benton completed his Bible college courses, he could officially pursue a career as a full-time minister of the gospel. He spoke seriously to me that night. "Margaret, thank you for everything. This last year was really tough with school, but you stood by me all the way. Finally, I am finished school. Now it is time to take the next step, and I cannot see spending my life with anyone else. Margaret, I love you, and I want us to set a wedding date."

CHAPTER 10

Marriage and Family

May your fountain be blessed,
and may you rejoice in the wife of your youth.
A loving doe, a graceful deer –
may her breasts satisfy you always,
may you ever be intoxicated with her love.

—Proverbs 5:18–19

Planning the wedding was a bit of a challenge. Benton wanted a big wedding, but we had no savings. Family, neighbors, church friends and my aunt who arrived from Guyana provided for our needs, and we had a lovely wedding ceremony.

My wedding dress was simple but beautiful, with a white lace bodice, scalloped neckline and long sleeves. My hair was styled in allover curls that tightly hung under the humble but elegant veil. Most of my sisters were bridesmaids, and the eldest of the bunch, Jennifer, stood as my maid of honor. The youngest, Faith, along with Benton's niece Marsha and a child from next door to our home in Bank Hall were flower girls. They wore beautiful pink dresses accessorized with gloves, simple veiled hats and dress shoes. My brothers were groomsmen.

The day was colorful and memorable. I cherish the black and white photos that are representative of the time we lived in. After the ceremony, we had a reception fit for a king and queen with a large buffet. The long buffet tables were all weighed down: there were deviled eggs, a bouchée hors d'oeuvres (pastry with a filling), curry seasoned chicken, filleted fried flying fish, green peas and rice and an array of vegetables to satisfy any palate, plus fruit punch and Bajan soft drinks like Juicy and Fruity.

Of course, at the end of the meal, it was time for Benton and me to cut the large traditional black cake. This wedding cake is made with a dozen eggs, flour and fruits that have been fermenting for over a year in liquor. The cake is very dense and covered with a hard, white, sweet sugar icing that covers a layer of almond paste. The almond paste fuses with the icing, making it taste good enough to eat alone. As traditional, Benton and I saved the top layer of the cake to freeze and eat during our first anniversary celebration. Overall, our July 14, 1962 wedding day was perfect, and we were very happy.

Immediately after the wedding, we left for a short honeymoon at Bathsheba, located in the parish of St. Joseph. The trip was paid for by my Aunt Grace. Our room was located on the ocean side, so we had a view of the beautiful beach and breathtaking sunrises. We were to stay for about a week. Each day over breakfast, we shared our plans for our future. Benton had great dreams and vision. He wanted to eventually start his own church. He could envision us traveling in the near future to other countries, perhaps even to England to visit my brother. We discussed buying a big house for the large family he wanted us to have. Benton was so proud to have a wife that he could not wait to take me to meet his father Nathan who had relocated to New York where he lived with his girlfriend. He had visions of grandeur and promised a great future where there would be nothing that was too good for our family. I felt so safe with him. I thought, *This is what it feels like to be in love!* With Benton now in my life, only great things were going to happen and together we'd bear the burdens of life.

We spent some of our afternoons on the beach, picnicking and tanning and now and then Benton took a dip in the ocean, but for me, my mother's warning that likened the ocean to the mouth of the grave was enough to keep me out of the water. Other afternoons we spent by the pool, where waiters delivered refreshing coconut water in freshly cut coconut right to our chairs. We were truly sprinkled with

VIP treatment. At sunset, we would walk along the beach holding hands. I remembered seeing this romantic scenario many times before with other couples. Now it was our moment to enjoy the romance ourselves followed by the union we affectionately awaited. The suspense was incredibly stimulating.

This new level of romance was exciting, but mysterious at the same time as I had never made love with a man. I never told Benton about my past with Daddy. It was not necessary. God was in our lives and our future was yet to be seen. I knew that the abuse pressed upon me by my father was not to be considered by any stretch of the imagination as a "previous experience." Instead, my feeling of responsibility to my husband overshadowed my reluctance, and even though I was afraid, I recalled my mother handing me a jar of petroleum jelly when I was packing to leave home. At the time I did not know what it was for, and she did not explain. But I quickly found out! That was the only conversation about the birds and the bees that I would ever have with my parents, but it paid off as the marriage night turned out to be very nice.

We had a wonderful honeymoon. But at last it was time to go home and face the everyday world. Early that morning we drove from Bathsheba to Black Rock, St. Michael. Finally, a flat in the parish of St. Michael to call our home! I was excited to return because I wanted to begin setting up our new residence. We had received some wedding gifts that were waiting for us to open and use right away, including curtains, kitchen items and linens. I was glad to have them, since I did not have any of my own to bring with me. Our good friend Pastor Barret contributed some furniture, including a beautiful dark brown bedroom set with a matching bureau, mirror, side tables and lamps. He provided a table and two chairs that we used in the kitchen. We were so glad to have all this furniture donated to us. After the expenses of the wedding, we could not have purchased any additional items for quite some time.

According to local customs, the mid-twenties was a very late age to marry. Most of my friends had married by age 21. But I knew that with all I had experienced, this was the right time for me. Benton and

I had a great future in front of us. After all the pain and disappointments, finally I had found someone to love and who would love me.

After some time in the role as Margaret Matias, I found myself pregnant. I was happy, yet very uncertain all at the same time. A new life was beginning to take form within my body, a breathing, living soul. When experiencing morning sickness, I recalled the scriptures about Mary the mother of Jesus and I looked forward to having a God-ordained family of my own. I read in Luke, "But the angel said to her, 'Do not be afraid Mary; you have found favor with God'" (1:30), and I was no longer anxious.

During the pregnancy I kept my job because I was still healthy enough on most days to continue working. During the nine months, Benton accepted assignments to preach at various churches of all denominations in different parts of the island. As my pregnancy proceeded through the second trimester, it became difficult for me to travel with Benton to his different engagements, but I continued to attend church, which was close to our home.

One Sunday, while Benton had gone to preach at a church, I went to an early appointment for a checkup with my obstetrician. I had planned to go to church after seeing the doctor; however, after my examination, the doctor asked me a few questions.

"Are you still employed?"

"Yes," was my reply.

"Mrs. Matias, you must resign from your position." His words were very firm, clear, and to the point.

"But doctor, the job I have is not very stressful. I am an accountant. I sit down most of the day. My income is very important to sustain my household. My husband does not have a full time job, so we need my job." Tears began to well up in my eyes.

"Margaret, if you don't follow my instructions, you will die."

That did it. I left the doctor's office in tears. Instead of going to church, I went back home.

The doctor's diagnosis was toxemia. It was the first time I'd heard that word. According to my physician, the disease is common with a first pregnancy. I was told that my blood pressure could continue to rise and cause me to have convulsions or go into a coma or ultimately die. I had no choice. I had to stay home and relax for the balance of my pregnancy.

I was all alone and crying in my bed when I heard a knock on the door. Without getting out of bed, I called for the person to come in. A friend from the church choir came to the house to check on me. I told her the details of the doctor's report and immediately she offered a prayer for me. Then she held me and told me that everything would be ok.

There was a Bible on my bed, and she picked it up. When she randomly opened the scriptures, there on the page before her was a verse that seemed to be just for me. "When he heard this, Jesus said, *'This sickness will not end in death. No, it is for God's glory so that God's Son may be glorified through it'*" (John 11:4). I was so happy that I lifted my hands to thank God. At this moment of concern, God's love comforted both of us when a friend had heart and cared enough to do something about it. Our spirits were lifted.

My custom on Sundays was to wake up early in the morning to cook dinner and have everything ready so that we could eat after returning home from church; however, after hearing the news from my doctor, I did not feel hungry, so I did not eat anything. I waited for Benton to come home to tell him the news. At about 5 p.m., he returned and was anxious to hear what the doctor had to say. He ate his dinner while I told him all that had happened. I was still not hungry so I decided I would eat later, when I was feeling better.

After dinner, we went into the living room where Benton could sit and relax after his long day. Suddenly, he said to me that he was feeling sick. I got very scared and asked him if he had eaten anything besides dinner. He hadn't. About an hour later, he began vomiting. I called my next door neighbor, who came over to help. But Benton was getting worse. Finally, I telephoned my father, who lived about a half an hour away. He came and took Benton to the hospital. The doctor's diagnosis was food poisoning.

Of course, it was dreadful that Benton had gotten sick. But I thanked God that I had not had an appetite, nor eaten any dinner.

Who knows what such poisoning and vomiting would have done to me and the baby? The next morning, Benton came home from the hospital. The pregnancy continued along on schedule until the ninth month, when I began to worry that the baby was overdue. The doctor insisted I had calculated wrong. But the ninth month ended without my giving birth, so surely the baby could arrive at any time!

Then one day, I began to experience a few intermittent cramps. Was I about to go into labor? To add to my concerns, the news was broadcast that a hurricane was headed for the island. I panicked. I was still not in labor. What if I went into labor during the hurricane? Benton was elsewhere preaching, so I called my sister to come over and stay with me. By the time Jennifer arrived, the intensity of what I thought were contractions appeared to increase. My sister stayed by my side. I began to feel faint when finally Benton arrived home. He immediately drove me to the hospital and during the drive, he did his best to calm me.

Once we arrived at the hospital, they rushed me to the examination room. To my surprise, my water did not break and I was not dilated. With the hospital filled with emergencies, they sent me to labor at home, but told me that I should come in the next day if my water did not break that night. The hurricane, named Flora, was due to hit the island. The newscasters predicted it would be the worst hurricane to hit us in over 100 years. Immediately, I prayed to God that He would make everything all right in our situation. Not long after, the hurricane turned away from the island.

Flora was one of the deadliest Atlantic hurricanes recorded. But we have a saying: "God is a Bajan." Many of our neighboring Caribbean islands are devastated year after year with the loss of property and loved ones. I was extremely happy that God was watchful over me and our baby, even in the midst of the storm.

The next morning, Benton drove me through flooded streets strewn with palm tree branches to the hospital, where they induced labor. I thought I experienced pain the day before, but now the times between rest and unbearable cramps were coming faster than I could cry out in hopes to mask the overwhelming degree of pain. Within a few hours and with a little help, I delivered my 9-pound baby girl. She was beautiful, with almond-shaped eyes like Benton's and a full head of hair. I was so happy that my first daughter, Barbara, was born healthy, without any complications. The nurse carefully placed her in my arms. I took hold of her little hands. Tears rolled down my face. This was a happy moment in my life and one that would be eternally memorable. Barbara grew quickly and was very precious, as most firstborns are. After all the years spent taking care of my siblings, I was happy to at last be taking care of a baby who really belonged to me. I was particularly elated that God healed me of the toxemia and that my body was healthy again.

***

I was learning so much about parenting my little angel sent from God when sometime after I was in the same condition. The spirit of life had breathed into me once again, and now my body carefully cradled a new soul. When my beautiful second baby girl, Chelsie, arrived, the long-awaited moment of joy was strong in the room. Perhaps later I would find it a challenge to take care of two young children at once, but for now, such thoughts did not worry me. I was very blessed.

My sisters, who lived nearby, were glad to lend a helping hand. It felt almost as if I had twins, with all the feeding and changing diapers and putting both girls to sleep on almost the same schedule. I dressed the girls alike and out of convenience I often styled their hair into long twisted plaits with matching ribbons. They were adorable. During a long afternoon service, the church mothers would frequently compliment me on how well-dressed and well-behaved my daughters were.

Just when I was adjusting to taking care of two babies, we decided to move to the parish of St. Philip. Then, a few year later, I was told by my doctor that I was "pushing breadfruit"—I was pregnant again.

My third daughter was born on my birthday. I had made all the usual special holiday dishes, baked cakes and decorated the tree before going to bed on Christmas Eve. Benton had asked me to wake him in two hours so that he could put the finishing touches on his

Christmas sermon that the Pastor asked him to share as a member of the local church. I set the alarm for 3 a.m., and when it went off, Benton left the room and went to the kitchen with his Bible.

While I intended to remain in bed, I decided to set out the clothes that we and the children would wear to church. But when I stood up, I felt a warm liquid run down my legs. I thought, *Oh God, not now!* After having had two children, it was clear to me that I was in labor. As the typical spasmodic pains had not begun yet, I continued on with the task of preparing to attend morning service. I really did not want to be in the hospital on my birthday—or Christmas, for that matter. But finally, I could not ignore the on and off stretch of abdominal pains that had begun. The familiar immobilizing moments were returning with shorter periods of rest time in between.

Benton walked in the room and realized what was happening. "Cheese on bread! You're having the baby!" he cried out. In a panic, he couldn't get the call through to the hospital, so I took the phone and placed the call. My contractions were now coming every five minutes.

The early morning hour and the fact that we lived a great distance from my parents made it difficult for us to have family members watch Barbara and Chelsie, so we had to awaken our neighbors. My friend came over to stay with the sleeping girls, and Benton and I left for the hospital. Benton dropped me off, checked me in and left to go preach his sermon for the Sunrise Service.

What are the odds of being born on Christmas day and having a baby on Christmas day? When this turned out to be the case, I was elated to be in the hospital on Christmas day! I was in labor for quite some time before fully dilated. The nurses were nice and jovial, and they made my holiday hospital stay enjoyable. They even broke the rules and allowed me to eat a piece of Christmas cake.

Crystal was born at 9 a.m., weighed 9 pounds 4 ounces and was healthy, with bright, sky-blue eyes and hair as golden as the rays of the sun. I could not believe this beautiful baby girl belonged to me! She was full of life. She offered a big smile whenever I smiled and said hello. I asked Benton to share with our neighbors all the baked goods I had made the day before. Ever since she was born, it has been fun to celebrate Crystal's and my Christmas birthday together.

CHAPTER 11

The Great Migration

The LORD makes firm the steps of the one who delights in him.

—Psalm 37:23

We lived in the parish of St. Philip until on one day in the year of 1967, Benton came home to say that he had some great news. "Margaret, we are going to America! It is the land of opportunity. We can do so much more and make so much more money. We need to pack up everything and go. I believe that this is what God wants our next step to be."

I had an uneasy feeling about the idea, as I was aware that Benton's father Nathan, who had moved to America, had been encouraging him to come to the United States. "Benton," I said, "what about our friends and family? And the children are so young. America is indeed a wonderful place, but it won't hurt for us to take time and plan so that we can do the move right."

"Margaret, there is so much I want to see and do. Come, Margaret. Look." He quickly pulled me outside and with a sweep of his arm, asked, "What do you see?"

"The beautiful fruit trees and vegetables that I planted," I answered promptly.

"You know what I see?" He looked deeply into my eyes.

"I see that I was born to reach beyond the borders of this island. With my contacts in America, I will go to the United States and preach. I want you to go with me, but I'll need to go alone and I will send for you and the children at a later time."

"Benton, please tell me you're joking. Right away?" I said, though I could tell very well that he wasn't. But I didn't like what I was hearing, and I desperately wanted his urgency to be a joke! I had seen Benton overcome before by zealous moments such as this.

"I'm not joking!" he said, more quietly, but just as insistently. "I've been thinking about this for some time now!"

"Benton, I know America is the land of the free and the home of the brave, but why move right now?" I objected. "You are getting more preaching engagements than anticipated. Besides, look across the way." Now I was the one doing the pointing. "When I am low on flour or cane sugar, I can just step next door and Ms. Carter is more than happy to give me a cup or two to meet our immediate needs. And there, on the other side of the luscious bed of green leaved coconut trees, is Mr. Cumberbatch, who helped you fix the car brakes just because he was blessed by one of the sermons you preached at church that caused his children to want to go back to church with him. Do you know how many times the church family just stops over to check on us and the girls, just because of the love in their hearts? And somehow, their visits seem to happen just when we need them most. Benton, these are the luxuries of a community that is very helpful to us with our three small steps apart children. If we are clear on the offering in America and take time to plan things out, that would make much more sense. God is not a God of confusion. We need time to prepare instead of rushing into a chance on an unspecified opportunity!"

"Margaret, I have family in New York," Benton reminded me. "They can be your new community. I am sure my Aunt Ella or Aunt Petunia or my father and his girlfriend will help us until we can settle on our own. They all live in Brooklyn, New York, so we have nothing to lose."

"We have everything to lose!" I disagreed. "Aren't we commissioned to do things decently and in order? Your dad did not come to our wedding. He neither called nor sent a card to say congratulations.

His girlfriend does not appear to be home very often as I've called several times to give her and Nathan an update about his three grandchildren. Benton! How can any good come of this without a plan. Did you pray about this decision?"

For a moment he had the grace to look ashamed. Then he puffed himself up again and said, "Margaret, I don't need to bother God about everything. I am a man of God! I understand when the times and the seasons are changing. Just like when Moses brought the children of Israel out of Egypt to the Promise Land. I will bring my family to America!"

He was preaching at me by then, but his voice quieted suddenly, seductively: "Margaret, did you know they have buildings that are so high in New York City that if you go to the roof of one of them you could probably feel closer to God?"

"Oh, really!" I made a face at him. "Well, remember in the Bible about the Tower of Babel and what happened to those people when they wanted to build a tower to reach God? Benton, I don't need to climb a building in New York City to see God. He is here, all around me, wherever I turn."

And just like that, Benton's soft voice was gone again. "I am not discussing this anymore, you hear? This is the end. Just have everything packed and ready to go when I say so."

And as far as Benton was concerned, that was that, and there was nothing more to say. I knew he was determined to pursue this venture, but even if I wasn't ready to concede, now was not the time to talk about it further.

For the rest of the evening I remained silent, keeping my thoughts to myself. I knew Benton had family in America, so it was true, we wouldn't be entirely alone there. But the thought of relocating to another part of the world in such an upheaval left me feeling uneasy.

***

The next morning, I awoke with the heaviness of Benton and my conversation on my mind and only found a peace of mind when I decided to say a prayer about it. I then grasped the family situation.

Benton made a choice, and given what he said, the girls and I would have many preparations to make for this trip. But how could I do it all – get ready for a move to America, to another country? Each day I ran a household and cared for three small children by myself while Benton went out to preach and teach around Barbados. Now, it seemed all the tasks related to moving to America had also fallen to me. Of course, we needed money to go there, and at this point in time it was Benton's preaching that brought in our income, so I could hardly begrudge him the time he was away from home earning his good will offerings. At this time Benton's popularity increased and most preaching engagements brought him referrals to preach at different churches. Any extra money received that did not cover expenses was put aside for the big trip that Benton agreed we would make on two separate occasions.

Benton decided to go ahead of us. He promised that he would take care of us and then came up with a plan. While away, he would work out our living arrangements in New York. The children and I had to move in with my parents in Barbados while Benton went on ahead to take care of things like establishing economic stability as a preacher. Once he was settled and had a place arranged for us — whether it would be our own place or one with his relatives, remained to be seen — he would then send for us.

My parents' home was very small. They had already agreed to harbor three grandchildren. At this point, one of my sisters had two girls and my younger brother a boy. Now, with my tribe moving in, the home was filled with six grandchildren all under the age of six years old. It was crowded, but I did not complain because my family was being very generous to have us stay with them. They were a big help to me during this transition.

Each day I collected the mail, anxious for news from Benton about his experiences in New York. I was usually disappointed. I wasn't surprised, though, as I remembered how infrequently Benton had written when he had been away at school. I tried to tell myself that this was just Benton's way. But it made me a bit uneasy, just the same. "Margaret, cheer up," my friends at church would say. "He is probably working hard to make sure everything is ready for you and the girls to join him.

"If Benton would just send the paperwork," I told my sister Faith one day, "I could arrange for passports. All I'd have to do, then, is just wait for the money and airplane tickets. But to hear nothing? I don't know. The children miss him. Every day they ask me when Daddy is coming home, and all I can tell them is that he will be back real soon to take us on the airplane to America."

Faith had her own opinions about Benton: "What kind of man would leave his wife and three children to fend for themselves?"

I tried to protest, but Faith continued. "Margaret, you are a beautiful woman. You know Mr. Parks down at the store? He said to me that you are a fine catch and that if Mr. Benton does not return, he may just have to take you as a wife, himself!"

"Faith, you are making up stories. He did not say that!" I declared, laughing a little.

"Well, you are pretty enough that he could have! Seriously, please listen to me, Margaret. Look at your situation now. A mother of three, practically abandoned! He has not called or at least written. Not one note to even say he arrived safely. We hear from Paris often enough. If it was up to me, I would just leave him."

"Faith, I love Benton. Why would I think like that? Besides, I'm more concerned than anything." I hurriedly suppressed any small doubts that might belie my own words.

Once I was alone, I couldn't help thinking that perhaps Faith was right. But I was loathe to admit it. I felt confused and was trying to sort things out by myself, but it wasn't easy. If only Benton were here! The ocean that separated us made it impossible for me to connect with him emotionally or spiritually. Thank God I had my faith and the love of my children and family to keep me while I waited to hear from him.

My sister Paris called me from where she lived on the east coast in United States. Paris had taken the opportunity to leave Barbados to attend university on a full scholarship. We had promised each other that we would stay in touch during her time there, no matter what. I was so proud of her. Paris had not disappointed the family. Her high grades kept her at the top of her class. I was so glad to get her phone call!

"Margaret, how are you and the girls?" she asked. "I was thinking about you this weekend, so I decided to give you a call just to check on you."

"You know me, Paris. I am holding on."

"Any word from Benton about the paperwork?"

"I am trying to be patient but he has not called nor even sent us any details."

"Margaret I think I know why. I received a call from Lance – from the church we went to as children. He moved to New York from Barbados long before Benton or I arrived here. He got Benton a job selling insurance."

"Paris, that sounds like good news."

"Unfortunately, there is more. Lance expressed an unsettling strong sense of urgency for you and the girls to join Benton in the United States but did not go into details. Margaret, you need special documents for you and the children to enter the United States. I cannot believe he did not contact you yet with the information."

"I know, it's been about a years' time since he left. I would have already taken care of it myself if I only knew where to begin!"

"I have looked into the details on this end and I will call you next weekend to tell you what to do," Paris promised.

"But what about money? I don't have a dime to buy tickets or prepare anything for the trip."

"Don't worry," Paris said. "I am working and am saving some money to help you. I was planning to visit Barbados this summer, but instead I will take on a few more hours of work during the week and that will make up the difference. I will have the money for your airline tickets. You stepped in and took care of us when Mommy couldn't physically do it anymore. It is the least that I can do. If not for all your sacrifices — helping me with my schoolwork and allowing me to study instead of doing the chores late at night... So don't worry!"

"Paris, I will make sure Benton pays you back every penny."

"Okay. But let's not worry about that now. I will call you next weekend with the details. Please tell everyone that I say hello and send my love."

My conversation with Paris had given me renewed hope – which was sorely needed because several more months passed without word from Benton. Eventually, as promised, Paris had earned enough money for the plane tickets and the needed paperwork, and she sent it to me. Although Paris lived very far from New York, at least she would no longer be the only family member in America. Now I could move ahead with the plan to join Benton in New York.

My sisters Faith, Jennifer and Yasmin helped me pack my belongings and made breads and lots of goodies for us to take to America. Coconut drops, fish cakes, flying fish, tamarind balls, guava cheese, cheese cutters and pone were just a few of the items that we carefully packed away in my and the children's suitcases.

The final days of preparation were difficult for me. This would be my first international trip, and though I kept up a brave face for the girls, I was really anxious, especially as I hadn't heard from Benton. I was leaving behind everything that was familiar to me. I was saying goodbye to all my friends and loved ones, as well as the church members who had been so faithful and good to me.

One afternoon I sat on my bed combing Barbara's hair in preparation for the going-away party my family had planned for that day. "Mommy," she said, "I am so scared to leave Barbados. I do not want to go. I do not want to leave all my friends."

I felt the same way! But aloud, I said, "Oh, sweetie, don't worry. I will take care of you no matter what. I love you." I hugged her tightly, comforting myself as much as I was her. I had to bury my true feelings for now, until I found a moment alone to face the coming reality — I hadn't quite managed to do this yet, but time was short now, and I had to deal with the fact that I was leaving Barbados, possibly forever.

Before joining the farewell party, I pressed my hand against the bedroom door frame for just a brief moment, took a deep breath and then opened the door wide to find everyone waiting for us in the living room. The welcoming smiles and hugs were so familiar, and yet they carried a sense of finality. I resolved to ignore an increased sad sensation that was causing my blood pressure to rise. I decided to enjoy the party and this time spent with friends and loved ones.

My sisters had prepared a meal fit for a queen and her three princesses! The familiar smell of curry, stew, steamed vegetables and fish filled the air. Tears, laughter, hugs and kisses could be found throughout the home all afternoon as we shared the goodbye meal. It was truly a poignant time. At some point during the party, I approached Daddy, hugged him, and without words let him know that all was forgiven.

Mommy was too arthritic to be up and moving around very much. She mostly sat in her wicker chair, watching the girls and me. There was a great sadness in her eyes much like what I had seen when Vincent was leaving for England and Paris the USA. I wanted to tell her I would be back to visit and would see her again, but deep in my heart, I knew not when. All afternoon, watching Mommy as closely as she was watching me, I sensed that this might be our final chance to hug and cling to each other in this life. As if my eyes were opened for the first time in years, I saw that Mommy had grown older and more tired. For these moments shared with Mommy, I was overwhelmed and truly couldn't come to grips with the reality that it was really time to say goodbye!

With effort, I brushed away the sad thoughts and concentrated on enjoying the last hours with my family and friends. They all seemed happy for the opportunity the girls and I had to go to the United States and better our situation, so I tried to be happy, too.

"Margaret," said Faith, as the youngest sister in our family, "I would like to share something." She stood in the center of the room where we had gathered. With all eyes on her, she looked only at me, her gaze sad and serious. "You have been like a mother to me. Without you, I would still be burning the fritters." Laughter eased the tension for a moment. Then Faith burst out, "I will miss you, Margaret! Please don't go!"

I stood to embrace my youngest sister. As I did, I gazed over her head at the rest of my family. It was suddenly clear to me that they really did not want me to leave, but like me, they were trying to be optimistic about this new development in my life. Despite being with them all for only few hours more, it was really at that moment that I was finally able to close that chapter in my life, knowing that I had the pure love of my family to keep my memories alive.

**

The next day Faith and her friend took my children and me to the airport. After boarding and making sure all the children were settled in their seats, I took a minute to pray for our safety during this new step in our lives. What would we find in the United States? Opportunity for financial security? Peace of mind? A better way of life? I was following my husband and I hoped he was following Jesus. I hoped — and prayed — that in time, all would fall into place.

"Please fasten your seat belts" are the words I remember hearing before we were in flight. Within minutes, we were airborne. I looked out the window to see my small island home, completely surrounded by water. All those years ago, I had stood on the beach envisioning my island, but now I could truly see it all from an elevated perspective. The communities — indeed, all of island life on Barbados — were so self-contained, so personal to me. It was one of the saddest moments of my life to watch my island home seemingly fly away from me as the plane moved farther and farther out over the sea. *Barbados, you were good to me*, I thought. But just as the island grew smaller and fainter in the distance, so did all my original hopes and dreams slip further behind me. The future was all we had. I prayed that it would be enough. The girls soon dozed off. I closed my eyes, too, and the next thing I knew, I was waking as the plane landed at John F. Kennedy International Airport in New York City.

It was around the winter of 1969 when we left the tropical weather, Barbadian island culture under the British Crowne, and arrived in the United States. My three young daughters and I walked off of the airplane and stepped into a whole new world. Throngs of people surrounded us, and I felt suddenly helpless, a stranger without friends or husband, as Benton was not going to meet us at the airport. Instead, he was sending his father. As Benton had never contacted me, I had given my father-in-law's information to Paris, and she had made the arrangements for him to pick us up from the airport.

I looked around to find anyone who might look like they could be Benton's father, wondering all the while why Benton had not arranged to meet us himself. Surely he wasn't preaching every minute of every day? I was so afraid. I would not know what to do if I could not make the connection here at the airport with Benton's father. There was no way for me to contact Benton, as I had not been given a phone number or address. Hoping that my father-in-law would forward mail to Benton, I sent him a letter two weeks before our journey to outline the details. I could only pray that Benton had received it. We were excited to see him and anticipated his joy to see us.

I was sitting nervously in the luggage pick-up area, the girls gathered close against me, trying to digest the vastness of the airport, when I saw a tall, confident-looking man walking toward us. Beyond a photo, I did not know how Nathan looked, as he had left Barbados and Benton to move to London, England where he got married and had three more children before divorcing and moving to America.

"Hello, are you Margaret?" he asked with a familiar sing-song Barbadian sound.

Surprised that my father-in-law would actually recognize me, I answered, "Yes. Hello, Nathan."

"These three must be your children. Come let's go, time's wasting, follow me."

And at that, he grabbed a couple of pieces of luggage, turned and started to walk away. It was an awkward moment, but I was grateful that he had come to pick us up from this new and unfamiliar circumstance. My heart racing, I hurriedly pulled together the children and our other bags, and we followed Nathan to his car, which he had left parked in front of the arrivals terminal. It was funny: when Nathan was putting the luggage in the trunk, I walked the children to the left side of the car. I quickly remembered that Americans drive on the opposite side of the road from the British custom. After putting the children in the back seat, I walked around to the right side of the car and sat in the front passenger seat.

As we drove away from the airport into Brooklyn, my mouth dropped with wonder to actually be experiencing how different the landscape was from Barbados. I had, of course, seen pictures of New York. But it was thrilling being there in person, watching the cars and people hurry along in the streets and on the sidewalks. Just as often, it seemed people rushed fearlessly into traffic to cross the street, as if playing dodge ball with the many vehicles. Most wore warm-looking coats, hats, and gloves to keep the evening chill at bay. I shivered inside my light jacket. The girls and I could not prepare for the cold northern climate, as coats were not needed in the Caribbean, so we were ill-dressed for our arrival in a wintry New York City. I was anxious to end the travelling and get out of the cold when Nathan turned onto Prospect Place, the street in Brooklyn where his home was located. He lived in a three story brownstone, so called as the outside was covered with small bricks arranged in neatly coordinated rows that created a beautiful pattern. The brownstone had sizeable floor to ceiling windows. At that moment, Nathan's home looked to me like a miniature mansion. Or perhaps it, like everything else starting with the airport, just seemed larger. The children's eyes were certainly wide open by this time.

As we followed Nathan up a set of tall, cement stairs, we held on to the metal side railings. In just a moment, I thought, feeling a flash of uncertainty, I would be meeting Nathan's girlfriend, whom Benton referred to as his stepmother. I had no idea what to expect, now that we were all invading their home. Nathan opened his front door and ushered us in.

The moment had come. I looked around for the mystery woman. She stood just inside the door, watching. My first thought was that she had a very kind face. Oddly, she seemed surprised to see the children and me, almost as if she hadn't expected us — or hadn't known what to expect. I never quite figured out that expression on her face.

Through all the formal greetings and handshakes, I kept glancing around for Benton. Where was he? Why wasn't he here? Then the phone rang. It was Benton, calling for me.

"Margaret, my car broke down," he told me. "I will need to take the train to Brooklyn."

"Okay. So you should be here soon?" I asked with anxious hope.

"I am in Poughkeepsie. No, I will not be there soon!"

He acted as if I ought to know how far away this Poughkeepsie place was!

"The next train won't arrive in Brooklyn for another four hours," he added.

Four hours, I thought! "So, what should I do until you get here?" I was feeling annoyed – and disliking that this was the tone of my first personal interaction with Benton .

But he didn't act as if this mattered to him at the moment. "Margaret, just make sure the children behave themselves," he said bluntly. "I said I am on my way."

"Okay, then. I love you," I added quickly, but the receiver had already clicked in my ear.

***

For the next several hours, I engaged in cordial conversation with my in-laws, just to fill the time until Benton would arrive home. The girls were too tired to join in, so I had my work cut out for me. Finally, at one o'clock in the morning, Benton walked in the door. I was very tired by then. We had not eaten much — though thank God Nathan's girlfriend had offered us a beverage and light snacks — and the children were now sound asleep. I stood up to greet him, arms opened wide in eagerness to see him after our year of separation, and expected the same from him.

To my utter disappointment and embarrassment, Benton neither hugged nor kissed me. We hadn't seen each other in almost a year! What could he be thinking?! Hiding my disappointment, I looked for any excuse I could give him. I decided to conclude that he must just be tired from his train trip from Poughkeepsie. Of course, I was being generous. The girls and I had just made a much longer trip under much more strenuous circumstances.

Benton had a strange expression on his face, like that saying, "He looks like the cat that swallowed the canary." In retrospect, that was Benton's expression exactly. But that moment wasn't the time to figure everything out.

At last — now that Benton was here — Nathan's girlfriend brought out food. We woke the children to eat. Conversation during this mealtime was sparse. The television in the living room helped break the silence until it was time for us to rest. The children and I were given a spare room upstairs on the second floor. The children lay on a blanket on the floor, and I took the twin-sized bed. Benton slept on the couch on the first floor. While eating breakfast in the morning and not knowing what our living arrangements would be, I was surprised to find out from Benton that we would be leaving for Poughkeepsie, New York. Wanting to respect my in-laws' home, I didn't ask any questions at that time. Instead I decided to follow my husband's lead.

After we ate, we got ready to leave. Nathan's girlfriend provided us with a throw cover to take with us so we would not shiver from the winter cold. Nathan drove Benton, the girls and me to the station to catch the first morning train to the place I by then knew was spelled as P-o-u-g-h-k-e-e-p-s-i-e. It seemed to take forever to get there, four hours at least. The trip was particularly exhausting for the children, and I began to forgive Benton a little for his earlier attitude at Nathan's. Traveling four hours from Poughkeepsie in the middle of the night would surely make anyone grumpy.

When we arrived in Poughkeepsie, we took a taxi to an apartment building. We passed a few individual homes on the way, scattered along a grass-lined road that reminded me, with some stretching of my imagination, of some places in Barbados. Our neighborhood seemed nice and quiet. Of course, it was the midday, and people were at work. We would know more later about our new surroundings, once the neighborhood came to life.

Benton and I carried the luggage and proceeded into the town-home-style apartment building with the children. By this time, the girls were wide awake and excited to see their daddy again. On the way to the apartment the girls were hugging and pulling competitively for attention on his legs. Benton laughed. For a moment, it felt like old times.

Inside, the apartment was scantily furnished. A brown sofa sleeper, and a four-person oak wood meal table with matching chairs were the only visible items in the dual living/dining room. Down the hallway was the bathroom and bedroom. The only covers waiting for the children were a sheet and two pillows on the floor. As it was midday by now, the children were using their first burst of energy after napping on the train to spend hours listening to their daddy tell stories and engaging him in playing hide and seek, as they ran around hiding in each room of their new home. I've always loved watching Benton interact with the children.

While Benton was spending long overdue quality time with the children, I took in our new home and daydreamed how I could decorate it to make our apartment feel more like home. I peered out each window taking in the suburban community. Then I began sorting the many items in our luggage making notes of what our home would need and wondering all the while if we would be able to afford such a long list of desires. The evening seemed to quickly approach, and the children were hungry. I used the food that we'd brought from Barbados to prepare cheese cutters, made with tennis rolls and Barbados cheese. I also cut up a golden apple and a mango that managed to make it through customs back at the airport. After their meal, the children became restless and were staggering on their feet. So, I decided to undress the girls to ready them for sleep — I couldn't help worrying that they would not be warm enough. I had not been warm since we arrived! Still, I did my best to settle them down for the night. We followed our normal routine of taking a bedtime bath, then I sang songs and told bedtime Bible stories. The girls loved this time so much and soon fell fast asleep. I arose from the floor beside them, fatigued from the day's events but happy to have some alone time with Benton. I staggered to Benton where he was sleeping on the pullout bed.

I entered the room with great excitement, ready to embrace the husband I had not seen for longer than was healthy for any young couple. I quickly undressed and crawled into bed beside him, reaching out to him — just to hear that he was snoring! I lay in the bed feeling so alone and wondering why in the world that I had brought the girls to this foreign country. But on second thought, I was really just annoyed with Benton's continued absence, even though he now lay next to me. The children were happy to be reunited with their father, but as I replayed all that had happened since our arrival, I couldn't help but recall the distance I felt from my husband. With this thought, I restlessly drifted into well-needed slumber.

To my pleasant surprise in the dark silence of the night, strong arms wrapped around me cradling me in their warm comforting embrace. I felt every nerve ending in my body was standing in a sensual readiness to indulge in the undefiled marriage bed, the anticipated ecstasy of the act of love between husband and wife was more vibrant than I had remembered it. Suddenly things changed, and rather unlike usual, Benton moved quickly, with none of the normal stimulations. We were thrust into the end goal of this intimate moment gone sour. Although disappointingly unfulfilling, without a word ever passing between us, he held me tightly, like his life depended on it. I thought he must have missed me desperately and as a result lost his customary stamina for a more engaging encounter.

***

I woke the next morning in our new home to my first sight of falling snowflakes. Of course, I knew about snow, but I'd never seen it with my own eyes – soft petals of frozen rain falling to cover the ground. A blanket of white soon covered the streets outside the apartment, as if God desired to clean the slate and give everyone a brand new start. Standing by the window, watching the pure whiteness cover the brown, withered grass, I decided to put the night's disappointment behind me by having a positive outlook of starting our new journey afresh in America.

When Benton awoke, to my surprise he began to get dressed right away. "Honey, where are you going so early?"

"Somewhere you would not want to go," was his response. There was a slight edge in his voice.

"I see. It's just that I was hoping we could spend some time together." I smiled at him. "The kids are still asleep and…."

"You should know that things are different now. My girlfriend will be here soon."

Had he just said what I thought I heard? "Your what?!" I laughed hysterically with unbelief. "What?! Are you crazy?! This is some silly joke!" I said. What else could it be, I thought frantically. "Benton, come here and stop playing games."

"Margaret, I'm not joking."

"You never sent for us as you promised! Is this why?" I reached out to get his attention, but he swatted my hand away.

"Woman, don't touch me. I told you I have to get ready."

"Have you lost your God-fearing mind? That's not what you said last night." This was perhaps the second most shocking moment of my life. I didn't know what to do, so I got busy getting dressed. I tried to talk to Benton, but he wouldn't talk to me. All I could think to do while the children slept was to put away the pullout bed. As a sense of unreality seeped in, I paced the floor in disbelief, unable to anticipate what would happen next. Praying to God for discernment, I thanked the Lord the girls were not awake for this horrible moment.

As the clock struck seven o'clock, the doorbell rang and Benton opened the door. There, against a backdrop of the hallway window, with the beautiful, pure snow still falling lightly to the ground, stood impurity personified. Benton's girlfriend stood beside him at the doorway entrance. To my amazement, he let her in and introduced her to me as his "friend."

I hardly knew what to say, so at first, I just looked at her. She was dressed in a simple black coat, black shoes and black wool gloves. Her hair was pulled back into a ponytail. My first thought was that she was dressed as if she were on her way to a funeral. She actually extended her hand, but contrary to my natural instincts, I ignored her gesture. This woman — whose existence I had not even known about until that very day — was willingly destroying my family; I had no desire at the moment to be cordial. What had Benton been thinking, to have this woman come here to meet me? What was his reasoning? Shocked, hurt and upset, I now know the truth behind the distance of thought and action – but what had possessed Benton to ever tell me?

I needed answers, and I didn't need them from Benton. I asked him to go to the bedroom while I talked with his "friend." I expected him to object and was surprised when he didn't. He walked away and down the hall without a word, leaving me in more of a state of confusion than ever.

I turned back to the waiting woman. "Your name again?" I asked.

"Brenda," she responded with a smile.

"Brenda, listen to me, and listen good. Benton is my husband. He is the father of my three girls. I don't know what he has told you, but you cannot see him anymore. Do you understand me?"

She simply stared at me, with her hands resting on her round belly as if she were a regular beer drinker, and as if I was speaking an unknown language. She then opened her coat to reveal her pregnancy and expressed that she and Benton were hoping for a baby boy. I was flabbergasted to see her smile once more. I really didn't understand this at all. Nauseated and speechless, I had the answers I sought and no more words for Brenda.

Benton rejoined us in the living room, where I proceeded to tell him that Brenda had agreed to my request — she hadn't, not verbally, but I couldn't imagine that she would continue to want to see Benton now that we arrived. But Benton had other ideas.

Turning to Brenda, he asked, "Did you promise her that?"

Brenda laughed. "No way."

Then, right in front of me, Benton turned to embrace Brenda, giving her a passionate kiss. With deliberate cruelty – only God knew why – Benton smiled at me and said, simply, "Goodbye, Margaret."

As Benton and Brenda walked away to leave the apartment, I remained silent and did everything in my emotionally-shaken being to reach out to my inner Christian spirit that was at the brink of erupting with cries for the Lord's mercy. Benton did not say goodbye to his children. Brenda looked back at me one last time, giving me a triumphant smile. Then they were gone.

I was alone! The girls and I had been abandoned in America with no one to turn to. Had Nathan and his girlfriend known about Brenda and the baby? Why hadn't anyone warned me? Why had Benton brought me to Poughkeepsie if he didn't want me? Didn't he care about his children? Whose apartment was this? Was it truly Benton's? Did she have other boyfriends that could be the father? Would he continue paying for the apartment, or must I immediately find a means to feed, clothe and shelter our children in this place where I knew next to nothing?

As I watched them walk to their car through the apartment window, a multitude of questions that brought a piercing chill to my soul raced through my head, spinning like the snow drifts I watched blow. I thought *What are we going to do?* as buckets of tears rolled down my face. I sobbed seemingly without end.

CHAPTER 12

Choose Life

God has said,
"Never will I leave you; never will I forsake you."
So we say with confidence,
"The Lord is my helper, I will not be afraid.
What can mere mortals do to me?"

—Hebrews 13:5–6

*L*iving in America, without any contact with relatives, I used the days to teach preschool and bible lessons to the girls. My evenings were spent praying for direction and crying hysterically from despair over abandonment and marital dishonesty. I rejoiced, however, as I had the word of God hidden in my heart. I had faith that this situation somehow would pass. Because I understood that God promised not to leave us or forsake us I had hope and the strength I needed to think about what I could possibly do to take care of the girls and myself.

There was nothing in the refrigerator but empty ice trays, so I was thankful for the extra food my sisters had packed for the children and me. If we had not had it, we might have been starving. I had no American money and didn't know when our situation would change, so I rationed the food with great care. There was neither phone, TV nor radio in the apartment, and we knew no one to ask for help. Painful tears of regret filled my eyes day and night for having come to America. If only I'd followed my instincts and told Benton no – or had just let him go and forgotten about him. These types of disparaging thoughts often infiltrated the camps of my mind. I waged a war to follow biblical scriptures like those in the book of Corinthians that reminded me to think on what is true, just and of good report. But of course, this trial made the effort almost impossible. I recalled how the girls and I missed Benton, so I had come to America. I had not known what else to do. But, now as a consequence of this faith in my adulterer husband, we were stranded. I was truly a stranger in a strange land, constantly searching my mind and praying with all my heart, desperate for some indication or inspiration of what I should or could do for the girls and myself. I was on the edge of despair when I endeavored to allow the Holy Spirit to "guard my heart and mind through Christ Jesus," that's when the miracles began to roll in.

On the last day of the week of our arrival, a salesman came to the door, hoping to sell me some of his wares. I didn't want to buy anything, of course, but in trying to refuse him politely, I mentioned that I only had Eastern Caribbean dollars in my wallet. To my surprise, the salesman kindly offered to convert my Caribbean money into U.S. currency. He explained that Benton was a customer of his. I assumed he was willing to help me as a gesture of customer goodwill. Whatever his motivation, his appearance at our door was miraculously well-timed. He estimated that my Barbados money was worth approximately fifteen dollars and made the exchange. Whether this was an accurate estimation, I don't know, but I was happy to have the American dollars.

As soon as the salesman left, I gathered the girls to go to the store. Although none of the girls had warm enough clothes to be outside in the bitter upstate New York winter, I didn't want to leave them alone, we had needs, and I had no choice but to go outside. We hurried through our errand and returned home as soon as possible with some badly needed basic items. We were so cold while outside I feared that we'd get frostbite before getting back to the apartment. Once back home, all we could do was sit and shiver for a long while until we became warm again. Oh, how I missed the warm sunshine of Barbados!

My heart and soul were heavy laden. What Benton had done was unforgivable. In some ways, it felt like we were being held hostage, but as much as I detested his choices, I knew we still needed him to guide us in our new American life.

Benton did eventually return. For the sake of the girls, I decided not to discuss where he had been for the last week. From that moment forward, I had to do what was best for the children, and staying with Benton was the only way I could take care of them. During his visit he drove us to the grocery store. I had been so caught off guard by his unannounced arrival that morning that I hadn't yet looked outside. When I opened the front door to leave for the store I saw that a new snow was falling. It had already begun to pile up on the street and was quickly redressing the neighborhood with a blanket of white that softened all the hard suburban edges. As we still did not have the proper clothing to go outside and remembering how cold we had been when running errands, I decided to put two layers of jackets and long pants on the children and myself, hoping to retain at least some warmth. Not knowing when next Benton would again return, we had to have groceries. I could only hope Benton would not keep us outdoors too long.

As I walked to the car, I reached out to catch a falling flake or two in my hand. Of course, each one melted as soon as it touched my warm palm. Silently, I compared the instantly melting snowflakes to the life I had expected to live with Benton here in the U.S. It had looked so lovely and promising from a distance, but had melted away as soon as it was within reach. This had been a truly heartbreaking week. As that day progressed, the snow slowly deepened over streets and sidewalks, bushes and trees, houses and yards to create a true winter wonderland to dazzle the girls and me. Having always lived in the Caribbean, we had only seen snow on television. Desperately longing for some form of comfort, I thought that if nothing else came from this atrocious migration experience, at least the girls had the chance to see this amazing element called snow. This blanket of white brought a smile to the girls' faces and seemed to have created a twinkle of joy despite the hard blow Benton had dealt us — of course, it was not enough to make me forget it altogether. I could look at my breath in the cold and appreciate the winter beauty around me, even in this state of despair, but I knew then that nothing would ever let me forget how Benton had neglected us. I knew for my own sanity, if nothing else, I would eventually need to forgive, even if I never in all conscience would be able to forget. I decided to leave this situation in the good Lord's sovereign and all governing hands.

On the drive back from shopping, I had a flashback of our prior island life. Whenever we returned from the grocery store there, I had always put away the food while Benton played with the children, keeping them occupied and out from under my feet, as well as taking the opportunity to spend some quality time with them himself. He would bounce the children on his knee and sing to them, or play spelling and riddle games. One of the girls' favorite riddles was about a man who lived on an island and had a mouse, a cat and a bowl of milk.

"The man had to take his cat, his mouse and his bowl of milk across the river on a raft to another island safely," Benton told them, "but he could only take one of them at a time. How did he get them all to the other side safely?"

"Daddy, he takes the milk, just in case he got thirsty," Barbara said.

"But then the cat would eat the mouse," Benton explained and on it would go.

There was always lots of laughter and fun as the girls took turns trying to solve the puzzles Benton presented to them. I enjoyed those times myself.

But when we returned from the store on this afternoon, Benton had no time for the girls. After we brought in the groceries, he soon went back outside in what had become almost a blizzard, to dig out Brenda's car that was then spinning its wheels. When he realized he could not move the car this time, as the tires just spun in the snow, he came back in the house, fussing and complaining.

"Margaret, listen. Brenda will be here tomorrow, so you behave yourself, you hear? I don't want any foolishness from you again. I have to drop her to work and then take her car to see my insurance clients."

I stepped up close to him, face to face, stood flat footed and said, "Benton, I don't want that woman in my house, do you hear me?" I tried to keep a steady voice, despite the nausea churning in my stomach. To think that I was standing here arguing with my husband about his girlfriend! If I had had a choice – if I'd known anyone else in New York or if I had the money – the girls and I would have been gone when he returned. But we were as good as stranded and at least for now at Benton's mercy. But I drew the line at entertaining his mistress!

Benton had other ideas. He said, "This is not your house. This is my apartment, and I will do whatever I want."

I was heated with disappointment and feelings of rejection. I thought, *My husband has gone crazy. He seems to have convinced himself that this is normal. How can he be so selfish to think he can do what he wants without any remorse for his actions?* For sure he was trying to push me away.

I walked away feeling disenchanted and dreadful. I continued in deep thought. What was I to expect from a preacher who had sinned and was not willing to repent? I couldn't believe it was happening. I wanted it to be a bad dream. Where was the man that heard from God to take me as his wife? I had to think about how to provide for my children and myself. Not knowing where to get a job or interim help was a paralyzing thought.

After a dinner filled with only the interaction amongst the girls, it was soon time for bed. That night, Benton and I laid at opposite ends of the bed, but this time he never touched me – and I was glad to not have had to deal with the contention. Nonetheless, with Benton lying so near to me, in such an intimate setting, I was heartbroken. In the still of the darkness, as I clenched my pillow and silenced a wailing cry, my tears rolled down my cheeks, falling onto the pillow like a torrential rainstorm – a rhythm, as if to match the rapid, distressed beat of my broken heart.

***

The next morning after digging out Brenda's car, Benton left to pick her up before the children woke, as if it were the most natural thing in the world. He gave no indication of when he was coming back or how the children and I were supposed to care for ourselves, and it was a long while before I saw him again. I wanted to call my sister or at least my in-laws, but I didn't have a phone. Then it came to me to introduce myself to our upstairs neighbors and ask if I could use their telephone. Although the neighbors were complete strangers to me, I was desperate.

Hesitantly, I approached my neighbor's apartment and knocked on the door. It opened to reveal a very pretty woman with a warm smile. She was dressed in a clean, pressed housecoat and blue slippers. "Hello, my name is Margaret Matias, and I live downstairs."

After a formal greeting, Dana mentioned how she watched me and the children walking to the store. She then said, "I make sure to always check when I hear people going in and out because sometimes the kids from across the street come over here to play hide and seek. Where are your Three Musketeers?"

"I would have brought my daughters with me but they are napping."

She gestured for me to come in.

My neighbor's apartment was furnished with simple and well-used furniture. The couch and chair were covered in a mixed-pattern fabric that was a bit dog-eared around the edges, as if a cat had clawed it. A very small television sat on her dining room table. The room was dimly lit, but the day's sunlight made a world of a difference.

"How are you adjusting to the neighborhood?"

"We are coming along, thank you."

"Where is Mr. Matias? I have not seen him for a few days. I guess he is off at his sister's house for the week?"

His sister's? Oh! I suddenly realized that my neighbor was referring to Brenda. But what husband would go off to a sister's house for a week when his wife has just arrived in America?

"Nice lady, that Miss Brenda." She pushed on: "I hear it was she who purchased the furniture and decorated your apartment for your arrival to the states."

I thought about the lavish furnishings in the girls' bedroom – two pillows and one thin sheet on the floor – and said nothing.

"Yes, you have a lovely sister-in-law. Not too many women these days would be so kind."

Yes, particularly women of that sort, I thought.

"But pardon me," Dana interrupted herself, "I tend to run off at the mouth a bit. How can I help you?"

"Well, I still have a lot to learn about the local stores, how to get around in the city and also what type of clothing is best to wear in this cold weather."

"Cold? Why, March can be the worst month of the winter season! They say we are due for another long winter. Temperatures often drop below single digits this time of year. You and the girls will be okay. Just be sure to wear a heavy coat, some kind of thick hat and some gloves. You do have a hat, don't you? Don't go outside without a hat! All the heat in the body escapes right through the top of your head, you know. You okay, Mrs. Matias?"

She must have noticed the worried look on my face. We came from the tropics, and we don't own cold-weather clothing."

"Well, you have come to the right place! Now that I have a grand-child that I help take care of, I don't get out as much as I used to, so I have extra coats that I don't need. They are bit old, and the lining is torn and my grandson's coats might be tight on one girl and big on the other, but at least they will help until you can buy something else."

"Thank you – Is it Ms. or Mrs...?"

"Please, just call me Dana."

"Thank you, and please, call me Margaret. Before I go, may I ask a really big favor? I need to make a telephone call, but my phone does not have a dial tone. Would it be okay if I used yours?"

Her expression changed to one of wariness. "Now, just hold on a second there, Margaret. I don't mind helping you out, but you know I have to watch my phone bill. Every minute adds up. Is the call local or long distance?"

"In Barbados it was one price to call anywhere on the island."

"Margaret, I have to know where you're calling before I can let you use my phone. For sure, I will not let you call Barbados. That is what we call an international phone call. The phone company charges extra because they have to connect you to an international operator. Can you imagine that? I cannot let you call international – that is too much. Let me see the phone number."

I handed her the folded piece of paper with the phone number I had for where Benton was working in New York.

"Okay," she said, "you are calling Manhattan. This is considered an in-state call, and it is not a problem. Next time I see Mr. Matias, I will just collect from him the cost of your call."

A short time later, I called Benton at the insurance company where he worked. I had a plan. I decided to speak to Benton and advise him of my desire to return to Brooklyn to stay with Nathan and his girlfriend. "At least there," I told him, "I can get around by bus and train." To my surprise, Benton agreed to come and pick up the family in a few days.

I returned to the room where Dana sat. There I expressed my appreciation for the phone call favor and the coats. I returned to my apartment, appreciative of God's merciful blessings that day.

***

The couple of days turned out to be a week, but at last, Benton came for us. The car ride to Brooklyn was very quiet. The children slept for most of the trip, and I did not have much to say to Benton. So, even though it was unlivable putting up with him, I would have to trust God and work with Benton to keep the channels open with the children. I wondered if Benton was forsaking the children and me the same way his father Nathan left after Benton's mother died? He was 5 years old, when a missionary family took him in and raised him. During that long ride, I planned to figure out a way to get out of this madness. My goal, I decided, must be to get a job so the girls and I could afford to live in America. This was a decision I never expected to have to make at this juncture of life and in a foreign country where I was woefully ignorant of the laws of the land – but I had to try. I had to do something to help the children and myself.

When we reached Nathan's house, Benton's stepmother came downstairs to speak with me. "Margaret, Benton tells me you need a place to stay. Nathan is in Barbados for several weeks. Before he returns, it's important for you and the children to find a place to live. Here is a local newspaper to help you get started. I hope you understand?"

"Thank you," I murmured quietly.

But my mind was racing as I realized the girls and I really were all alone in New York and had only a short time to figure out how to make our way on our own. The clock was ticking. Benton slept over that night – then he left early the next morning from his father's house. That was the last time I saw Benton for a very long time. Knowing we could only stay at my father-in-law's temporarily, I did the only thing I knew to do. I prayed – desperately. Soon thereafter, I met a young lady who lived with her dad and son on the third floor of Nathan's house.

Karen was in her early twenties, very smart and ready for the world. As we quickly became friends, she proved to be a great help to me.

"Margaret," she would say, "I know it seems hard right now, but you can make it. You don't need a man to define you. Remember, you are the role model for your girls. Be a woman they can respect and honor. A powerful black woman – that's who you are."

I noticed that Karen always stood tall and held her head high. "You are so confident," I told her. "It seems like nothing can hold you back."

"Margaret, I was not always like this," she confided. "There was a time when I was carefree and in love with a man who, I was sure, was the one for me. Later I found out he had another girlfriend, just around the corner. I was mad! I told him to get out. It was over. Yes, it hurt, and yes, sometimes I miss loving arms holding me at night, but never again with him. O-U-T! That's what I told him and there he went. I sat down, examined my life and decided where I wanted to be in five years. Being left behind by an irresponsible man wasn't going to be where I'd end up. I already have one baby and do not want anymore."

"But what about love. Don't you miss it?"

"Margaret, I am twenty-two years old. I will finish my business degree in one year, and I plan to continue and get my Master's. I don't have time for the neighborhood 'boys' and their petty ways. I will only settle for a real man who is on my level and can handle a shared life together."

"Karen, I may be new to this country but I have faith that if I can find a job and a babysitter for the children, I will make it in America."

At that, I broke down. I thought furiously, *If only Benton was not an adulterer!* I really thought he cared. I didn't understand how we could have had such a wonderful relationship in Barbados, only to have it disappear here in New York. But then, I admitted, a part of me had known, even back in Barbados, that our relationship there hadn't been without its flaws and questions. But it didn't matter. Right at that moment, in retrospect, it seemed like the only good times I'd ever had with Benton were all lies. Now I only felt abandoned and alone in a strange city, in a strange country. For the first time since my arrival, I stopped trying to be strong, and I cried until I could not cry anymore.

Karen hugged me as I wailed. She encouraged me and told me that I could make it on my own. "You have those beautiful girls," she reminded me. "So giving up is not an option."

She was right, of course. To help each other, we decided to take turns watching each other's children as we looked for employment.

On the days I went out to search for work, Karen loaned me tokens for the subway, since I had no job and little American currency to purchase tokens. With my considerable accounting experience, I hoped to find a job rather quickly. However, after several unsuccessful interviews, I suspected that my experience as an accountant in Barbados might not translate well to accounting methods used in America. I was almost ready to give up when on the day of my last scheduled interview, I was told of another job opening I should investigate. This job opportunity was farther away than I had traveled on my own so far. As I walked toward the subway station, I considered my situation. Should I pursue this lead? After all, my supply of tokens was running low. I might use too many of them investigating this far-away job and – if my previous job interviews were anything to go by – it would most likely come to nothing anyway. On the other hand, I had no other job prospects, nor any accessible family members in New York beyond Nathan, as I did not have contact information for Nathan's sisters Petunia and Ella. (They were both married to Caucasian men and lived somewhere in Brooklyn near the Verrazano Bridge.)

As I thought about a solution and prior to making a decision, I descended from the cold street corner and stood on the subway platform between the south and northbound trains. A sense of being overwhelmed crept into my spirit when I wanted to pray. Flabbergasted by thoughts of what train to take next and upset by my situation in general, I could not focus on my prayers.

The Bible talks about the adversary that tempted Eve in the Garden of Eden to humanity's demise. I believe that the adversary was the catalyst to Eve disobeying God and that the same evil lurks in the modern earth to tempt or discourage people today. In that moment, I was no exception. Despondent with no income and realizing that I had missed my menstrual cycle twice, the realization that I was pregnant with Benton's fourth child from our one night stand in Poughkeepsie was crippling. Suddenly a totally overwhelming feeling of helplessness rushed into my mind. I irrationally thought that the best solution for everyone would be if I just ended it all by jumping onto the train tracks as one of the trains raced into the station. Why bring another child into an already stressful situation? I imagined the last sound I would hear on earth would be the screeching sound of the train. *Once you're dead,* a darkly reassuring voice seemed to whisper, *the police will find Benton and he will have to take care of the children. You have no other choice!*

In that moment the tempter wanted me to give up, no prayers crossed my lips nor thoughts of Bible scriptures entered my mind. Instead, I looked down the long dark tunnel where I could see the headlights of the next train as it barreled toward the station. With my heart racing and sweat pouring down my face, I took a deep breath and moved slowly to the edge of the platform, as if led by some unseen but insistently grasping hand. The sound of the train grew louder as it drew near. I closed my eyes and prepared to lean forward onto the train tracks. Simultaneously, I was startled by a tap on my shoulder.

Opening my eyes, I whirled around. No one was near me. It was as if I were visited by an angel from God! Then the comforting Holy Spirt of God brought to my memory the scripture, *"The* LORD *watches over you—the* LORD *is your shade at your right hand; the sun will not harm you by day, nor the moon by night. The* LORD *will keep you from all harm—he will watch over your life; the* LORD *will watch over your coming and going both now and forevermore"* (Psalms 121:5–8).

I was filled with the awesomeness of God. Although I was befuddled, I believe God gave me clarity of thought in that moment and instantaneously I was overtaken with the presence of the love of the Lord. It was as if an angel was dispatched to comfort me and I was now safe.

I held myself tightly and sat down on the closest bench. The train arrived, let off its passengers, took on new ones, then closed its doors and pulled away again. I sat and stared at it, but I didn't really see it. I was blinded by God's love. I had just been given a gift, another chance – I knew then without a doubt that God hears and answers prayers. Tears first rolled slowly down my cheeks and then streamed. I cried feverishly and was not embarrassed. All my thoughts were now of God's love and his individual attention to each of his children young and old. Even when I did not love myself, he sent an angel to comfort me. I thought about my girls and how much they loved me and I them. I knew they would need their mother. My foolish suicide would have been the worst thing I could have done to them, had I succeeded.

Before I made another step, I prayed to God for his forgiveness. Like Eve, I had been distracted by the tempter. But thanks be to the grace of God, He saved me yet again. With my revived faith, I continued to go to Jesus for strength as I was so tired. I don't know what to do. "Please, God, make a way. I need your help." I sat a while longer, crying tears of thanksgiving. Then finally, I rose to return to my father-in-law's house and my dear children, filled with a renewed sense of hope. More days would pass without any new job leads, but I was determined to stay optimistic, despite knowing that my father-in-law would soon be due back from his trip. I had restored faith in God's grace, He had a plan for me and the children.

***

The next day, I took a phone call from Lance, a long-time friend from the church in Barbados. Lance was concerned and had called Nathan's home to find out why Benton had not come to work for several days. As we talked, Lance told me his cousin was giving up his position as an accountant in the city and suggested that I apply for the job. I was so excited! I got the details from Lance, thanked him profusely, and immediately called to arrange for an interview.

Then I went upstairs to give the good news to Karen, giving thanks to God all the way. Karen was thrilled for me, and she happily watched the girls for me while I went for the interview. The position was with a medical group located in New York City and only a thirty-minute train ride from my home. My interview went well, and I was hired immediately.

I couldn't have been more pleased with my new manager. He was a professional, charming man who trained me thoroughly in the role of properly managing the books for his division of the company. It was a challenge but I faced it and succeeded.

Not long before I found my new job and during my stay at Nathan's, the girls and I had found a friendly neighborhood church to attend where I met a lady who was so kind to share information about a family-friendly apartment located one block away from my father-in-law's house. This space had a living room, two bedrooms, one bathroom and a full kitchen. I calculated that two weeks' pay would take care of the rent. Nathan's trip had been extended by a few weeks, so I had extra time to earn money and make arrangements with the post office, utilities and the phone company – another blessing! Just days before my father-in-law returned to the States, the landlord agreed to divide the security deposit over three month's rent, allowing the children and me to immediately move into the new apartment,. Finally, things were working out. I had left Nathan's house without incident, and hopefully would never be dependent on Benton again. I was extremely happy. I now had a place I could call my home. The lady who rented the apartment to me provided a full-sized folding bed for the two eldest girls, and I managed to purchase another smaller bed that would serve for Crystal and me. The apartment was small, but it was home. Thank God for his love and promise of protection and the gift of life.

"This day I call the heavens and the earth as witnesses against you that I have set before you life and death, blessings and curses. Now choose life, so that you and your children may live."

–Deuteronomy 30:19

At last, I received my first paycheck, which was exactly two weeks' pay. There was more good fortune to come. I soon met a neighbor who lived below us, a Jamaican lady named Mrs. Emmy. She was a retired nurse and a sweet strong lady with a kind heart. The first time we met, she greeted me and the children with a big hug. "Whatever you need dear, no problem," were her very first words to me. Mrs. Emmy babysat the children in the neighborhood to supplement her fixed retirement income, and I was surprised when she offered to watch all three of my girls for the price of watching just one. This was a perfect arrangement for me, one that I could afford. She even had me bring them down in their night clothes, and she would dress them and feed them breakfast. This helped me to get going quickly to work in the mornings.

Having her as a friend and neighbor was a great blessing that gave me a wonderful sense of peace and security during my time at work, knowing that my girls were in good hands was a much appreciated blessing from God. Mrs. Emmy also raised her granddaughter, so in return for her generosity, I took her granddaughter under my wing so she could enjoy many play dates with my children and travel with me as one of the family to church. In the children's later years, Mrs. Emmy's granddaughter also enjoyed participating in many family events including the first family skit presented during a Sunday morning church service.

After some time at the medical group as an accountant, I was finally able to purchase a bit more furniture at a very good price. At last, my apartment was starting to shape up and looked properly decorated. At each of the windows where I had previously hung sheets for a bit of privacy, I now had curtains and pull down vinyl blinds. We used inexpensive sheets and added simple but adequate comforters on the chilly nights, so our bedrooms were cozy and welcoming. We all really loved the bathroom, where I had created a wonderland of pretty and pink everywhere, including a shower curtain with matching soap dish, toothbrush stand and garbage pail, as well as a shag rug and a fuzzy covering for the toilet. For mealtimes, I purchased a simple dinnerware set with matching glasses and silverware. I wanted my children to learn at a young age the proper way to set a table and how to use utensils.

I could tell things were working out. While the girls missed their father, I created the opportunity for telephone communication with him. I would encourage the girls to call Benton to help settle the differences they would sometimes have as siblings. I felt it was important to keep their father in their lives. Overall, the girls were happy. They would greet me with big hugs when I returned from work and share with me all the wonderful games and stories Mrs. Emmy taught them. Mrs. Emmy was so responsible. When the eldest girls were school age, Crystal would tell me how she and Mrs. Emmy would look out the window every day to watch out for Barbara and Chelsie as they held hands to walk to and from the public school that was located a short distance from our apartment building. I was so elated and thankful to God for His goodness and His mercies towards us.

***

One morning while I was getting dressed for work, the phone rang.

"Hi Blossom."

My heart skipped a beat – but only one. I took a breath and said carefully, "Benton, I am on my way to work. How did you get my new number?"

"My father gave it to me."

I didn't have words to say to him, so I remained silent.

"Margaret, I miss you and the children."

"I am sorry Benton, but I can't talk right now. I am running late for work."

"Margaret, I would like to come back and be a real family with you and the children. I know it is hard for you to raise the girls all by yourself."

I couldn't believe what he'd just said – nor did I believe he meant it. "Benton, I have to leave."

"Margaret, I was in a terrible car accident here in Poughkeepsie. I have been lying here in the hospital, just thinking about you and the kids. I really miss you. I really want to get back together with you once I am discharged from the hospital."

I gritted my teeth. "Benton, I cannot take the time now to talk about this. I must be on my way to work."

He talked on as if he hadn't even heard me. "Margaret, we should start a church in Brooklyn. I am sure that with all I have experienced, I can be a better leader. I just need another chance."

I'm sure my silence spoke volumes.

"Listen," he persisted, "I am no longer with Brenda. We broke up. But that is not why I want to come back. I really believe that God is calling me to start this church, and I want you by my side."

"Benton, I must go. We'll talk about this later."

I hung up and hurried out the door, but I thought about his call all the way to work.

I had been extremely shocked to hear his voice on the other end of the phone. He was right. It was very hard raising the girls by myself and he did not know that I was pregnant. I did prefer the children to grow up having a close relationship with their father. So, I spoke with him several times on the telephone and I made it clear that I was appalled at his actions and his lack of love for us. I asked him how I could be sure that he would not leave us again and that he was truly sorry. He simply promised not to and said that he knew then he couldn't run a church without a Godly woman and the mother of his children by his side. I didn't fall for lines so similar to what I've heard from him before. This time his persuasive argument appeared more to be around the church than his love for me. Benton with his charm and charisma had made promises that were not honored. I learned to lean on God's eternal promises that provide strength for today and bright hopes for the future. God promises a new heaven and earth where the city's streets are described as being paved with pure gold. Halleluiah! (Revelation 21:18–21.)

I thought about what might be best for the children. In my heart I forgave Benton as I would want God to forgive me, though forgetting would be obviously unlikely and a challenge. So, with sympathy and love for family dominating my decision, instead of saying no, I relented and agreed to take Benton back.

He arrived about five days later with a small suitcase, no job, and not even a promise of employment. All he talked about, or seemed to want to do, was to start a church. Taking part in such an endeavor was impossible for me. I had a job to go to and a family to support, and shortly there would be one more mouth to feed.

Benton wanted me to quit my job and help him start his new church, but I knew if I did, we would hit rock bottom for sure. I wanted to delay opening a church, and I asked him to go find a job first. Benton rapidly pursued starting a church instead. As we had no brick and mortar building in which to open a church, we moved to a bigger apartment which we needed for our growing family and simultaneously used this new space to start holding church meetings in our home. Each week by word of mouth, members would come to our home to worship God. Benton was back to his charismatic self, sharing the word of the Lord from the Bible. Benton was truly gifted in memorizing scriptures and applying the principles and presenting them in a form of storytelling that helped the congregation better understand the King James Version of the Bible.

I didn't want to quit my job, but after praying about the matter and having a newborn due any day, I thanked my boss for the wonderful opportunity he'd given me and with regret told him I would be resigning. It was a chore to hold back tears on my last day as I reflected on all that I learned and the great relationships I had formed with my coworkers, whom I would sorely miss. But, all I could do was put my trust in God and believe that everything would work out with the new church plans underway.

***

One day in the early 1970s, sharp labor pains awakened me. Benton rushed me to the hospital, where I delivered an 8 pound 14 ounce baby boy whom we named Benton Matias, Jr. My husband was ecstatic and dancing all over the hospital, announcing, "I just had a boy." I laughed to myself as he announced the birth as if it were his solo accomplishment. I hoped with all my heart that little Benton might be the missing link that finally tied our family together. I had given my husband a son.

So now we had four children, and my husband and I were both out of work. Finally, the congregation – a group of very loving Christians – outgrew the apartment. Growth is always a good sign of a healthy church. Although I enjoyed the intimacy and convenience of hosting church at our home, I was just as happy to have our church move to its own building.

As soon as we could, we found a building to move our church into. We called it the New Testament Church of God and held services every Sunday. I was humbled to be a pastor's wife and overjoyed to have the opportunity to use all the experience and training I had received in Bible school to help build the kingdom of God.

As the church expanded over time, it required greater finances to maintain the space and pay staff. Since the membership's tithes were not enough to keep things afloat, I decided to go back to work. The economy was ripe for hiring and I soon landed a job at the Metropolitan Museum of Art as a keypunch operator in the mail order department. I developed meaningful working relationships with my colleagues. My accounting background allowed me to be promoted to department supervisor after just a year on the job.

Benton established a visitation program through which he and his church aide, a young woman named Veronica, visited absentee and ailing members. This seemed a great opportunity for my husband and the aide to show their concern for the church's sick and shut-in members.

After working as a supervisor for a few years, we decided to rent, with the option to buy, a three-level brownstone house just a few blocks away from my father-in-law's house. Our three bedrooms were located on the second floor, so our daughters collectively and son could have their own rooms. The third floor of the brownstone was occupied by a different tenant.

At this point, everything in our home was going fine, but we needed a car.

"Benton, don't you think juggling, family, church life and work would work better if we had a car?"

"Margaret, I'm glad you said that. I have been looking at new car deals in the papers. I think we can do it. Come here look at this fleet of new car listings."

"Benton, unfortunately, buying our first car new doesn't fit our current budget."

"Blossom, let's look for used, then. Here, today's paper is highlighting a good deal on a Buick Skylark."

"Now that is much more affordable."

Needless to say, having the convenience of a car made life much more manageable. Unfortunately, the devil didn't like this trend of us stepping out on faith time and time again.

***

A day came when I arrived home from work to Benton rushing out of the house without conversation. I was met at the front door of our brownstone by my four-and-a-half year old son. He put a finger to his lips for me to be quiet and beckoned me to come to the bathroom. There, he whispered to me that earlier that day, while his sisters were in school, Benton had brought a lady named Veronica to the house. He had told Benton Jr. to stay in the family room and watch television and then he and Veronica had gone into Benton's and my bedroom and closed the door.

I was surprised that little Benton (Junie) was perceptive enough to realize something was wrong with the scenario his father had created and also that he instinctively told me about it in private. But foremost, I was furious with Benton – not only for obviously being unfaithful to me again, but also for conducting himself in such a fashion with his own young child watching television in the same house! I was desperately hurt as I realized Benton was back to living his double life. After all God's blessings, Benton practically turned his nose up at the Lord by doing such a horrible thing – in our home, in our marriage bed.

Without hesitation, I went upstairs, dragged our mattress all the way downstairs and threw it out into the backyard. At that moment, still standing at the back door, I heard the front door open. Benton had returned.

"Margaret, where are you?" Benton called.

"I'm in the back," I answered.

"I had to run out for a minute," he said as he approached. "What are you doing back here?" He joined me at the back of the house.

Then he saw the mattress lying in the yard. "Margaret, what in the name of tarnation are you doing with the mattress!"

"I decided we needed a new one so I'm throwing this one away."

"Why didn't you just wait until the new one arrived before throwing this away? And why are you throwing it away? There is nothing wrong with this mattress!"

Benton acted puzzled, and perhaps he was. Maybe he really believed I wouldn't find out about his philandering.

"Well, I really want a new one," was the only explanation I would give him.

He walked away, shaking his head and looking perplexed.

Later that week, I placed a lock on my bedroom door to prevent Benton from being able to open it and take Veronica in there when I was not at home. I mentioned that with a four, eight, ten and eleven year old, it would be best not to allow the children to have access to our room when we were not home. As there was only the one key and I kept it in my purse, I no longer had to worry about feeling invaded in my own bedroom.

"Sister Veronica" (*sister* and *brother* are titles used to greet people who are a part of the family of God) came to our house often on Sundays and ate dinner at my table many times. People would not be able to imagine that I sat and was cordial to the woman who was having an affair with my husband even if I told them under oath. Nevertheless, I didn't dare let Benton know I had found out about him and Sister Veronica, for fear he would punish our son for getting involved in grownups' affairs. Despite his usual laughing and joking manner with the children, Benton was a disciplinarian and would rule with a strong backhand lash or with a belt if the children ever were disrespectful or misbehaved. If he knew that Benton Jr. had told me about him bringing Veronica to the house, he might get angry enough to give our son a good lashing. So, I could do or say nothing to let him know I was aware of how he was carrying on with Veronica.

This went on for many months. Each Sunday, Sister Veronica would come to my house, greet me with a kiss and smile in my face, knowing that she would soon be stabbing me in my back yet again. At this point I had severe trust issues when it came to Benton's dealings. I would mentally question all of Benton's evening visitation appointments planed with Veronica, which often started with Benton picking

Veronica up from her home. My only comfort was when I prayed about what to do. As a result, I moved away from my customary mode of hospitality and told Benton that I would not be entertaining any longer. Yet they continued their routine visitations and Benton started staying out very late.

One morning, around the 3 a.m. hour, I was dreaming that my husband and I were walking in the park on a sunny day holding hands, like old times when we made our footprints in the white sands of the Barbadian seashore. This time however, we were strolling along a grass lined path that guarded beds of lilacs and pink orchids and tall cherry blossom trees. All of a sudden, as if my hand had turned to ice, he let me go. The sun and Benton slowly faded away. Although I called for him, his faint voice trailed away into the darkness that aggressively encamped around me. I came to a fork in a road and froze. I was astonished to see an enormous black rattlesnake coiled up and awaiting its prey. As I had been taught by my brother Vincent, I stood completely still and watched this humongous reptile uncoil. Its head became more and more visible, when lo and behold it was the face of Veronica, the pastor's aide. Startled, I jumped out of bed in a sweat and went downstairs to tell Benton, whom I thought had fallen asleep on the living room couch. To my utter surprise, he was not there. I pulled back the red drapes of our living room bay window, and I saw the car was gone as well.

Still very puzzled by my dream and unsurprisingly upset by my husband's absence, I went to make a cup of tea. Concealed behind the wall that divided the dining room from the kitchen, I sat down on a chair in the dim lighting from a small lightbulb located over the sink. I sipped hot, soothing Earl Grey tea. In the silence of the early morning, baffled by the irony of the moment, the slow turn of a key in the front door pierced the calm. Sitting quietly, I heard Benton enter the house then timidly creep down the hall. When I heard squeaks from the hallway's walk-in closet, I hesitantly peeped around the wall to see him changing into pajamas that I was not aware he stored there.

Pondering Benton's actions, I continued listening as he gingerly walked up the stairs. With the distant sound of the creaking of wood as he stepped on the fourth stair, I was able to envision his opposite foot raised, just above the fifth stair when the dedicated church office telephone rang. Swiftly moving to answer the phone, I beat him to it and quickly asked, without question of who the call was from: "Sis Veronica, why are you calling at this time of morning?"

With a frog in her throat she said, "Hello, Sister Margaret. I just have a quick question about a Bible verse that I need to pass by Pastor Matias."

Of course from my silence she may have sensed that I was not buying her story. Abruptly, Benton snatched the phone out of my hand. All I heard was "uh-huh." He said nothing that made sense or had any biblical reference. When he hung up the phone, he did not say a word to me. He just went upstairs.

I returned to the kitchen seat and wallowed in self-pity. *How could I have married such a traitor of a man of God?* Then I bowed my head and closed my eyes. Motionless, my warring thoughts paradoxically turned in the direction of appreciating God's sovereignty. In that concerning moment, I thought about all that was good in my life. In the midst of it all, I prayed that God would remove the mountains in my life and until then endow me with the grace, courage and strength to climb them. Having placed my burdens in the Master's hands, I could then go to sleep.

When the sun came out the next morning and we and the children gathered around the breakfast table as was customary, it was clear to Benton and me that we had begun the process of growing apart as communications between us remained scarce.

Meanwhile, my faith in God would not be shaken. My conversations with God developed a rapid fervor and as I would pray for direction and study the Word of God. Indifference to the mental anguish made room for the building of intense faith.

I am your servant; give me discernment that I may understand your statutes. It is time for you to act, LORD; your law is being broken. Because I love your commands more than gold, more than pure gold.

–Psalms 119:123–127

CHAPTER 13

Tragedy Amidst Traditions

For unto us a child is born, unto us a son is given,
and the government shall be upon His shoulder.
And his name shall be called,
wonderful, counselor, mighty God,
everlasting father, the prince of peace.

—Isaiah 9:6

When I lived in Barbados, Christmas Eve was always a very special time for my siblings and me. When I lived in Brooklyn, my four children enjoyed our joyful traditions. The children were "in charge" of the holiday decorations, which were packed away out of sight for eleven months of the year. Dragging out boxes of tinsel and other items, the girls would carefully unwrap the most fragile ornaments while Junie pulled out the red fluffy stockings. Singing along with the Christmas carols that played loudly on the radio, all the ornaments and stockings would be hung one by one on the six-foot green plastic tree we had set up in the corner of the living room. Within no time, the living room would be transformed and filled with joy of the Christmas spirit, complete with big smiles, warm hearts, homemade snowflakes on the windows, stringed popcorn on the tree and the smell of pine wreaths throughout the home.

Normally I would be in a very happy mood, whizzing around my kitchen preparing the holiday meal. The big day was Christmas Day itself. Christmas morning was carved out for the entire family to get dressed up in festive holiday dresses and suits to attend Christmas morning service for an 11:00 a.m. start. When we returned from church, I'd just need to add the finishing touches to the holiday meal. This process allowed dinner to be on the table around 3:00 p.m., but the preparation of the meal did not go off as customary this Christmas Eve. Early that morning, my routine was brought to an immediate stop when I realized that the light in my bathroom was not working. As I made my way around the house, it wasn't long before I realized that none of the lights were working. I took out my flashlight and went to the basement only to find out that our furnace was not working. As Benton was not home, I recalled him assuring me over the phone that he had paid the bills for this month, but nothing appeared to be wrong with the fuses or light bulbs, so what else could the problem be? With simmering annoyance, I looked out the front window, hoping that there wasn't a long term power outage that was affecting the neighborhood this joyous holiday morning. From the lights shining brightly through the diamond and rectangle glass shapes on the neighbors' front doors and windows, it was clear that the lighting issue was unique to our house. I then thought, *This house has a thirty year old furnace. Maybe it also has an older electrical system.*

I called the electric company, but they had no workman to send out on Christmas Eve day, so it looked like we were going to be without power. Imagine losing electrical power and heat on Christmas Eve! Unfortunately the winter cold had kicked in early that year, but thankfully, I was able to use the gas stove to warm up the house and cook meals while the sun was out. After all of my stove top cooking was complete, the evening crept in. Because I had no lights, I couldn't effectively see to function in the kitchen. I then thought to finish my baking of the cakes, ham, roast and other foods I had been preparing for the holiday at my father-in-law's home. After calling, they consented, so I packed up all the ingredients and pans I needed to complete the dishes and planned to be on my way as soon as Benton returned home.

When Benton arrived home in the early evening, we discussed what could have caused our electrical problem and he promised again that he paid the electric bill. As there was no solution in sight, we stopped discussing the problem and decided to bring the children's beds down from upstairs and place them onto the kitchen floor. We turned on the gas stove and opened the oven to heat the kitchen area. Since it was a very large space, we had adequate room for each bed with walking room in between. The kids thought it was fun to sleep in the kitchen. I lit long decorative holiday candles to help the children find their way in the dark if they needed to go to the bathroom. I strategically placed candles on top of the refrigerator, the kitchen counters and table.

I left my husband on duty to watch for the children's safety and headed to my father-in-law's house. On my arrival, I quickly greeted all their guests and proceeded to the kitchen. While cheerfulness arose in the living room, I focused on getting all the baked goods into the oven first. The cakes and coconut breads – our traditional custom – sent a sweet aroma throughout their home. As I pulled them from the oven, I was surprised that the alluring smell coming from the kitchen didn't cause the room to be stormed by Nathan's guests.

Next, I placed the ham and roast into the oven so they could finish cooking as my home oven was serving as a space heater. About an hour or so later, I called Benton to let him know that the baked goods and the ham and roast were ready, although the chicken now in the oven was not. To my dismay, there was no answer. Perhaps he had fallen asleep, I thought. It was almost midnight, after all. I called again, but still there was no answer.

Despite the late hour, Nathan's friends had not gone home. I could hear the laughter and singing coming from the den and knew that glasses of rum punch, beer and bourbon were being passed among them, fueling their long-winded conversations. I didn't want to bother Nathan, but as I continued calling home without getting an answer, I was becoming more and more anxious.

Finally I went into the living room where my father-in-law was partying.

"Nathan, excuse me," I said hesitantly.

"Margaret, whatever you're cooking in that kitchen has been the talk of the party." He took a big gulp of his Guinness Stout.

"Thank you. Since that's the case I'll leave a sweet potato pie for you all to enjoy." After the show of appreciation I interrupted again. "Nathan I am very sorry, but I really need your help."

"Yes?"

I gave an apologetic glance to his guests. "Would you mind stepping into the kitchen for a chat?"

Nathan's sharp annoyed look was discomforting and brought a chill to the festive spirit. He rose from his seat. Thankfully, he walked soberly.

"I am almost finished cooking and will be ready to go home in an hour. I have repeatedly called Benton to let him know because it is very late. He's probably sleeping because I get no answer, and given the situation at home..." I went on to express the potential risk with the children sleeping in the kitchen.

Nathan then said, "Come on quickly, and I will drop you."

"Thank you so much."

As I was putting my coat on, Nathan called for me.

"Margaret! Stop coming and come!"

I chuckled to myself. *Now I know where Benton gets that from,* I thought, and I ran outside.

The night air was very cold. I pulled my coat in towards my body and wrapped my arms around myself in a tight hug to hold out the chill. Nathan dropped me off and left to return to his home.

***

I opened the large wooden door to my home and quickly rushed in to escape the stony cold of the dark night. I hurried to check on the children. Confirming they were okay, I rushed upstairs to my bedroom to see if Benton was sleeping. To my surprise, he was not there. He had done some horrible things in the past, but I didn't think he would leave the children in danger. I called his name loudly as I checked the other bedrooms and bathroom.

I headed back downstairs to the kitchen, where the children remained sleeping. Just as I entered, a glass candle holder on top of the refrigerator shattered into pieces. Instantly, fire began to spread. I screamed to wake the children and pulled them out of harm's way. Quickly, I put out the fire before it could engulf the room.

I threw the broken candle pieces into the trash with my gloved hands. It was a while before I found all of them. Behind me, my children were crying as they realized the close call they had. Fear and anxiety colored my voice as I spoke to them through a loving, calm quiver of a voice that indeed settled them down. But all I could think was, thank God for His mercies! If I had not heeded the instinct to go home to see what was happening there, I might have lost my four children to fire!

After I got the children back to bed – I sat in the chair by the window to wait for Benton to return. Anxious and worried, I pulled back the curtains at every sound from the street. With each passing moment, I tried to understand how Benton could have left his children alone and unprotected. What was so important that he would put it before making sure that his family was safe?

About two hours later he came home.

"Benton, where were you?!"

"What's wrong now, Margaret? I was not gone for long."

"Benton? I know better than that!"

"Don't raise your voice to me."

"Oh, I will do more than that! Your children almost died in a fire because of your irresponsible choices. I asked you if you would watch over the children, and you said yes."

"I was hungry, and I wanted something to eat. You left no food for me."

"What foolishness are you saying, Benton? Why didn't you warm up leftovers? No, you were hungry, but not for food."

"What do you mean?"

"I saw you get out of Veronica's car, Benton. Just stop the lies. I don't want to hear them anymore." Then I said sarcastically, "Thank you for ruining Christmas. "

***

Crystal's and my Christmas birthdays were a disaster that year. I could only be grateful that my children had not died in a fire and we did not all fall ill after sleeping for a few days in the cold.

As the months passed, Benton continued his philandering. Oh, he always had a different story and a different excuse, but the outcome was always the same – he was neglecting his family and his responsibilities as a man. Although Benton liked to make what he called fritters for himself and the children (sweet fried dough seasoned with cinnamon and vanilla essence), he unfortunately didn't always keep the children safe. The truth always comes out, The electric company later confirmed that the bill Benton claimed to have paid for the month of December was not paid.

Everything came to a head one evening. After work I needed groceries, so I decided to walk to the local grocery store to buy a few items. The bags were heavy, so I took my time strolling to the house. On my way, to my stunned surprise, our Buick drove past with my husband at the wheel and Veronica beside him. I believe Benton must have seen me, but he never stopped to relieve me of my packages. But then, what else should I expect? He had another woman in the car, after all!

I walked on home, unloaded my groceries, made dinner and sat down to wait. When Benton finally arrived home late for dinner, I was fed up with him. For the first time in a long time, I didn't try to hide my resentment, even if it meant he would lose his temper and threaten to leave. I felt obligated to stay with Benton for the sake of the children and did a fine job of keeping these situations from them, but the mental abuse had become extremely overwhelming.

From that point on, things only got worse. Benton began sleeping out more frequently. At times, he would come home Sunday mornings to get dressed for church and take the children to Sunday school.

I suspected he was living with Veronica on those occasions. But the person really didn't matter at that point. That Sunday, I decided to fight the good fight of faith by trusting in God's promise of protection and in a nonviolent way push back. I no longer wanted to live in Benton's shadow of adultery. I decided to leave the church.

The hard part would be separating from the members I'd grown so found of as they were dear to my heart. Prayerfully, I thought, with me gone, they will discover the truth. The members would become inquisitive and finally find out the truth.

"Margaret, are you and the kids ready for church?"

My response was a cold silence.

"Margaret, do you hear me speaking to you."

"Benton, the kids and I are not going to your church with you this morning. Matter of fact, we are not going back to your church at all."

Little did he know I found another church to attend.

CHAPTER 14

Closed Doors & Opened Windows

I know your deeds.
See, I have placed before you an open door
that no one can shut.
I know that you have little strength,
yet you have kept my word and have not denied my name.

—Revelation 3:8

The Church of the Nazarene's building was large with a basement, second floor and a beautifully decorated sanctuary with stained glass windows and traditional solid oak pews. This foundation of the spiritual atmosphere lined the mezzanine and balcony levels. This Church of the Nazarene used a yellow school bus to pick up children for Sunday School, which was a very nice convenience for the children as I didn't drive.

Benton was angry and embarrassed that his wife and children now attended a church other than the one where he was pastor.

"What will I tell my congregation?" he demanded.

"That's something you're going to have to figure out. Benton, they are not blind. They must know what is going on. What you are doing is wrong in the sight of God, and I don't want to be a part of your charade anymore."

I was disappointed in all that was happening and with a sober mind realized it was time to take action. We needed a strategy. Even though Benton drove our car, I was actually the one who purchased it. I was grateful that I worked a full-time job every day and with that income and the well-intended offerings Benton received from the church members' donations, we were able to sustain the family, but finances were tight. I discussed with Benton that we needed to sell the car. He was upset but there were no other options that made financial or practical sense. The alternative was that Benton would commute on the New York public transportation system and I would continue to take two trains to work and back home again. The car had become a luxury.

Once the car was sold, Benton was furious. "Margaret, where is the car? Do you hear me speaking to you?"

"Benton, we talked about selling it and now that it is sold we can afford to pay the rent for both our home and what's owed on the church building monthly."

"You did what? You know I need that car!"

"We talked about this, so don't be mad that I followed through."

"I need the car."

"For what, Benton? To meet with your girlfriend? I am tired of you leaving this house whenever you want and coming back at all hours of the morning. I am sick of it. Do you hear me?"

"Margaret, don't speak to me like that."

"Benton, this conversation is very uncomfortable. I clearly have the sole burden of trying to keep us out of bankruptcy. We need to work together until we can afford another car."

Now at this point Benton had gone into his virtual man cave and was the one not talking.

"Benton, this conversation has made me sick to my stomach and now I am tired and am going to bed."

After a few more nights of Benton and I arguing about his late night rendezvous, Benton moved in with Veronica.

***

Some time passed before I heard from him again. However, I did hear from a few of the long-time members who'd started when the church was held in our home. They'd call to tell me how much they missed me and to ask when we were coming back. I guess initially it appeared as if I was the "bad guy." Eventually, the calls came in as sympathy calls. Then due to the truth of the matter, they shared that our church had dissolved. No one knew where Benton had gone.

Despite the uninvited heartache of a turbulent marriage, all that I experienced during those years with Benton made me stronger in my faith in God's divine grace. My children gave me the energy to move forward. As soon as possible, I moved to another apartment on Eastern Parkway in Brooklyn. It was a lovely large space with four bedrooms. From our new front window, we had a beautiful view of the sparsely tree-lined streets, bordered by park benches where we could sit and relax after a long day.

The neighborhood reflected a wide ethnic variety, including predominantly people of Jewish religion, Catholics, Protestants, Italians, African American and West Indians. Each year during the Labor Day holiday, people swamped the streets to watch the West Indian Day parade, where West Indians (from Barbados, Jamaica, Trinidad, Guyana, etc.) come together to represent their native Caribbean island. Each wore their colors and the music was bold and loud. Colorful floats, steel bands and groups of scantily clad dancers would make their way along the route. The sounds of calypso and reggae music triggered memories of the Crop Over Festival in Barbados. The children loved this time of year and loved watching the parade from the living room window. Of course, they were not allowed outside among the crowd because of the heavy drinking among the spectators.

When I lived on Eastern Parkway, I had an opportunity to help a middle-aged woman who was about 5'5" in height and who wore wigs most of the time due to hair loss. This hardworking woman had a cordial demeanor, a dark complexion, an unusually large, strong-looking frame and hands that were used to take care of the elderly. As she could not afford a place to call her home, I had my daughters share a bedroom so she would have a room of her own. Although she often stayed overnight with her ailing clients, when she did sleep in our home, the children didn't like it as she'd have to pass by the breakfast table each morning with her white potty held over head while cordially pleading for a pardon. Being an overweight lady who could not get back to sleep if she turned on lights to go to the restroom in the middle of the night, she would squeeze past the narrow space between the wall and the breakfast table chairs carrying the urine-filled potty from the prior night. During these notable moments, the children would hold their breath from both odor and fear of a spill, but it never spilled. She was welcomed to stay at our home for however long as she needed, and as she was kind to us, all the children adjusted.

I really loved our apartment, even though it was located on the fourth floor. Benton Jr. started attending the elementary school conveniently located nearby. The train that I took to the Metropolitan Museum of Art was just two blocks away. However, I noticed it was becoming more and more difficult to walk up those four flights of stairs. My knees felt more strained with each step. *I am getting old*, I thought.

Reluctantly, I began looking for another apartment. I found a two-family apartment near King's highway in Brooklyn, N.Y. that had just one flight of stairs. Even though the rent was higher, I was excited to find this space located on a block with three other families who also attended the Nazarene church. I considered it another blessing from God to have found a two-story house near other families that my children already knew.

To my excited recollection, my sister-in-law's mother Vivian and her family also lived in Brooklyn. Vivian's son-in-law Brian had a van, and with their help, we would be able move from Eastern Parkway. The children were excited to move to a neighborhood where they would be closer to their friends from church. Unfortunately, the move was not until late at night when my in-laws were available. To make a difficult situation worse, it was snowing. But, knowing laughter is the best medicine, we made the best of it given the weather conditions. After everyone had finished loading the van for its final trip, the van driver came to the door to help me take my last walk down those icy steps. We journeyed toward the warmth of the van, which beckoned us with the hum of its steady running engine. My children were safely tucked away in the back seat, huddled amongst the neatly arranged garment bags of clothes and in front of walls of furniture in the cargo area of the van.

As we approached the van, to my horror, it started moving! I could not imagine why this would be happening. Snow was on the ground, but the road was not a downhill grade. With a cry, Brian left me and began to chase his van, now gaining speed as it raced along the street. The road was very slippery, and I was afraid something terrible was happening, but all I could do was watch and pray as the van driver ran toward the vehicle and my precious children. Just then, the van seemed to swerve, and turning unexpectedly, it ran straight into a big tree, caving in the side of the van.

To all of our surprise, two unknown men jumped out and ran. Apparently, the thieves had taken advantage when Brian's back was turned. They'd hopped in to steal the van. If not for the snow, the thieves would have my furniture and children. Thank God they drove too fast on the slick street and when the van came to an abrupt stop, the thieves ran off without incident nor injury to the children. Thank God for taking what the devilishness of man meant for bad and for turning around the outcome to be in our favor! I believe God works in mysterious ways unknown to man.

When the driver checked, my children said that they had not noticed the strangers, and that they felt fine. The belongings were safe, and we proceeded to our new apartment without further difficulty. I decided this would be the last time I would move. Moving was such a hassle.

***

As time passed, we were even happier to have moved to this apartment, as the children were now experiencing a strong Christian foundation, which I value as undoubtedly important. I was pleased to see my children quickly forming strong bonds with other church members from the youth choir and the teen fellowship group. I, too, became very involved with the Nazarene church as a volunteer and gained support from the comradery among like-minded, God-trusting believers.

This was a growing church, made up of Americans and migrants from various Caribbean islands. The diversity footprint included Jamaicans, Trinidadians, African and Caribbean Americans, Guyanese, Barbadians – and these were just some of the cultures that made up the base of our local congregation. The parent Nazarene church that we often fellowshipped with was located in Kansas City and was predominantly Caucasian. Each year, the Nazarene churches would plan summer youth camps and national conventions that provided activities and workshops that presented the members with a chance to come together and learn more about the Bible and how to better help each other. In this way, we all got to know each other very well, and I felt at home.

After a few years, I was voted into the position of leader for a group called the Willing Workers. This group, predominantly women, raised funds to help with the church fuel bills and the building fund. Our most popular fund-raising projects included our annual bus outings to Pennsylvania to shop at outlet stores and to visit an amusement park. Participants – sometimes whole families – purchased tickets from our committee to join us on these trips, and whatever profits we made after travel expenses went into our church fund. As a bus excursion leader, the night before a bus trip, I always stayed up late to cook things like fish cakes, chicken, peas and rice and corn beef cakes to share with the members who signed up to ride on my bus.

The year of 1978 was different, however. The night before our planned bus trip, I was home, cooking as usual, when a call came from my sister in Barbados to tell me that our father had passed away. I put my head down for a minute as I thought about the bad news. My mind raced back to the day when I was on the beach with Daddy. I had not thought of that moment for many years. I was at a loss for words because of all the good Daddy had done for the family. I was also dismayed that a tainted image of him existed and immediately came to my mind. Nevertheless, I did not cry. Finally, the door was closed on that part of my life forever.

I continued to make the food for the bus trip and with each turn of the fish cake batter, the pain of my past was blended from a sticky doughy mix to a solid palatable finish. The following morning, my friends on the bus said, "Margaret, these are the best fish cakes I ever tasted."

Although I attended my mother's funeral when she died in her early 60s, I did not attend my father's funeral. I told the family, truthfully, that my job responsibilities in New York prevented me from being in attendance. Deep in my heart, I really did not want to be there. My sister Faith called afterward and shared the details of the funeral. She mentioned that Daddy was asking for me before he died. I did not ask Faith many questions, careful to keep my past state of relationship with Daddy distant from my current state of peace. I moved forward with work as usual.

It was a busy time at work, and I was fortunate to be placed on a fast track of promotions. My supervisory position was one of the most rewarding experiences in my life. It was wonderful to work within such a successful and well-known non-profit organization and it was an opportunity for me to learn and grow. I was responsible for hiring, training and firing. I took my work seriously and did my best to ensure that any task I was responsible for was done properly. I sometimes supervised and managed as many as twenty-two workers at a time, especially during the holiday season, when additional mail order staff was hired to support the increase in catalog gift orders. With this hiring demand, in addition to others, I placed my sister-in-law's sister and a family member of one of my neighbors who were seeking immediate employment. These hires worked out very well at the Met and many went on to hold long-term positions for many years.

The commute to work during the winter holiday season was challenging. I lived in a "two-fare" zone that included taking both a bus and two trains. With the delays from snow-covered roads and additional holiday shopper traffic, my commute to work from Brooklyn was easily two hours each way. On winter days, the wind would often whip sharply around me as I walked from the train station to 84th Street and Fifth Ave. I commuted on this route for at least 10 years until the museum moved its distribution office to Queens, where I remained until retirement. However, the daily trip to this new location took even longer – nearly three hours each way. There were more bus changes, and the walking portion was much farther. Making my way to this Queens, New York location tedious, but during the winter weather, getting there was often treacherous.

***

One day during this time, I was at home when my doorbell rang. I opened the door to find a strange man with a large envelope in his hand. He asked me to confirm my name, gave the envelope to me, then left in great haste. Turning the envelope over in my hand, I noted an official emblem of some kind on the outside. Feeling uneasy, I closed the door and went inside to open this mysterious package. Sitting on the couch, I took a deep breath, broke the seal and pulled out the cover letter. The top heading revealed that the state of New York was serving me with divorce papers. How could Benton do this to me? We had agreed when he sent the first set of papers that before I signed he would give me the down payment on a house. This had not yet materialized, though I had taken the initiative to call and remind him of his promise.

Then, barely two months later, this certified letter arrived with another set of divorce papers drawn up by a different lawyer. This time I sought legal counsel who advised me to go ahead and sign the divorce paperwork. The lawyer said he would charge me only a small fee for his services. *Well,* I thought, *Benton is insisting on a divorce and is committing marital unfaithfulness. I've done all that I could do. I will continue to trust God to guide and direct the children and me.*

I was grieved that it had finally come to this. I really loved Benton. God had worked beyond Benton's shortcomings to allow him to be a blessing to others. After all the good that came from his life when he preached, it appeared Benton was motivated by self-gratification.

The children were old enough to understand what kind of man their father had come to be. We were on our own for many years at this juncture in life. My only concern was that Benton Jr. (Junie) had not had a chance to really get to know his father. I felt it was important for the children, especially a son, to know his father on some level. But I had to admit that the time had finally come. Our marriage had been stressed for an unwholesomely prolonged time. I resolved that I would have to be both mother and father to our children.

Since my children were still in public school, from the 4th grade through high school, I decided not to remarry or even date. I didn't want to chance a man coming in and treating them inappropriately in any way. Besides, another man in my life would only cause more problems for me and the children. If the children became attached to a new man and things didn't work out, it would only confuse and hurt them again. Benton was their father and would always be their father regardless of my relationship with him.

With all this in mind, I signed the divorce papers. One of the clauses stated that Benton would pay me a certain amount of money per child as support for their future. Of course, he never did. At that time, I was unaware of my options within the legal system. I learned much too late that I could have taken him to court for neglecting to pay child support.

Within a few months after the divorce, Benton moved to Florida and remarried. His second wife Pat already had two teenaged children of her own. Benton helped Pat's oldest son by purchasing a car for him and later a record store. As a person with Christian values, I kept my conversations with Benton civil and I encouraged the children to call their father on his birthday and all the major holidays, just so they could keep in touch. The children could expect a call from their dad if they behaved badly. In partnership with his wife, Benton did eventually become a successful businessperson. They opened an assisted living home in Port St. Lucie. After success at this location, they opened another senior home in Fort Pierce. Pat was a nurse and very helpful with managing patient care. The business was successful but neither the children nor I ever received any money from Benton.

After some time, Junie grew into a handsome and caring young man. I was concerned about his companions and the type of person he might become as a result. The environment in our neighborhood was changing, and the young men with whom Junie was friends had very definite ideas about what made a person a "real man." "A real man is hard and aggressive." "They don't take any crap from anybody." "If they hit you first, knock them out so they'll think twice before trying it the next time."

Junie wanted to be cool and a part of the in crowd. I recognized the peer pressure he was under from his friends. As a concerned parent, I contacted Benton and together we arranged for Junie to visit his father in Florida for the summer. This turned out to be a great time for Junie as he connected man-to-man with his father. He finally had a chance to bond with his dad. He also took karate lessons. Benton Sr. purchased a large dog for our son, and I allowed Junie to bring it back to our apartment in Brooklyn. Because of his Karate training, on his return Junie appeared much taller, more confident in his speech, manner and overall approach. Unfortunately, Benton Sr. never did send the court-mandated child support payments. Neither did I decide to fight him in court.

His new marriage did not work out for very long. As I understand it, he walked away from the marriage, taking nothing from the one assisted living business that remained. Again, he was out of work.

CHAPTER 15

From Victory to Victim

Trust in the LORD with all your heart
and lean not on your own understanding;
in all your ways submit to him,
and he will make your paths straight.

—Proverbs 3:5–6

C hristmas 1981 – New York City was brimming with beautiful window displays in all its stores, each one more exciting than the last as all tried to top each other. I looked forward to this time of year. I would take the children to see the festive window displays. They *oohed* and *aahed* at it all: the sound of Christmas cheer, the creatively decorated trains, the pine trees and happy-looking families of mannequins dressed in seasonal colors and brilliance, ignited by moving mechanical magic. The season heralded a shared birthday for my youngest daughter and me, so we felt we had double blessings at Christmas time. It was easy to pretend that the lights sparkling everywhere transported us into a winter wonderland.

This year, however, was a Christmas my family and I would never forget – and for very mixed reasons. One afternoon deep into the holidays, I was downtown without the children. Crowds were everywhere – people shopping, traffic honking, Salvation Army Santas ringing bells on every corner. It was both exciting and hectic to walk about the hustle and bustle of the city. On this day though, I was not sightseeing. I was running an errand. Before going home, I decided to brave the holiday retail crowd. The yellow taxi cabs lined the streets as the flurry of people wove their way through oncoming traffic. Cars were everywhere, starting and stopping in fits across all the lanes.

The store I wished to visit was across the street from where I stood. Finally, the light turned green, and the walk signal winked its permission for me to proceed. I cautiously stepped off the curb to cross. At that instant, a car ran the red light. I was already in the crosswalk, and the car struck me, knocking me down into the slushy, snow-filled street. The driver put the car in reverse and rolled over my leg a second time before fleeing the scene.

Stunned, helpless, I could do nothing but lie in the street, cold and wet, encased in a severe pain that started in the base of my foot and shot relentlessly to the top of my neck. Through my tears, I saw a crowd gathering around me. Able only to move my eyes, I looked from face to face, wordlessly imploring that someone, anyone would help me. Silently, I cried to the Lord, *Why now? Why me?*

At first, no one did anything but stare as I lay helpless on the chilly pavement. The numbing shock from the impact began to wear off. My pain grew worse, and I was conscious of the cold winter air on my face. A handsome Caucasian man hurried and knelt beside me. Without hesitation, he took off his coat and covered me. As he bent over me, I looked into his eyes. Somewhere within my fragmented thoughts, his eyes reminded me of the beautiful blue Barbados waters. They were peaceful eyes and they looked deeply into mine as if to send me a silent message that everything would be all right.

The man stayed with me. He kept patting my cheek and asking if I could hear him. He turned to the crowd and requested that someone get blankets. Fleece blankets soon in hand, this good Samaritan replaced his coat with them, tucking them snugly around me. Soon after, a team of paramedics arrived. The good Samaritan had stayed with me the whole time. Now, unexpectedly, he kissed me on my cheek, wished me "Merry Christmas" and disappeared into the crowd.

I have never forgotten the feeling I had while this man knelt by my side, and I have never been able to properly describe it since. I only know that while it seemed odd that a stranger would treat me with so much kindness, it was also comforting and just what I needed at just that moment. Despite the pain of my injuries, I will always remember that encounter with the good Samaritan as a gift from God. It was a genuinely caring experience from a male.

The rescue squad took me to a hospital close to my home in Brooklyn. The doctors there examined me. My leg was broken and I sustained various other injuries. I was told later that when my children received the news of my accident, they became very upset and cried terribly. Thank God for my church neighbors, who kindly communicated to my children that their mother would be all right and brought them to visit me in the hospital. I had to stay in the hospital for three weeks with my leg in traction. The medical staff at the hospital was very kind. The doctors and nurses stopped by often to check on me. Since it was the holiday season, they allowed the youth choir of my church to stop by my room and sing a few Christmas Carols.

Finally, I was allowed to go home wearing a cast. I was so happy once I was back in my apartment. The church members welcomed me with flowers and frequently stopped by with meals and Christmas gifts for the children. As I was on sick leave from work for three months, I was gratefully appreciative when so many showered our family with compassion. During this time I reluctantly had to lay down while my children tended to the household duties not taken care of by my friends. This situation often brought me to tears as I remembered my mother when she was crippled and how, as a young girl, I had to take care of her. I had vowed that my children would never have to experience the difficult life I had as a child. My girls were so loving and supportive. My oldest, Barbara, would prepare the meals and comb her sisters' hair. The second, Chelsie, would organize the clothes for everyone to wear to school. My third and youngest daughter Crystal would help with the house cleaning and kept the girls' shared bedroom neat and clean. Benton Jr. would take care of the dog and make sure his room was clean.

Reflecting back on this time, I wish I could adequately thank my friends and loved ones for easing the physical and mental hardship that my accident brought to my family that year. We could not have gotten through that time without all their help and care. Their spirit of generosity warmed our home like a great cedar wood fire. Indeed, it could have been a very sad and difficult Christmas for us that year, but it didn't turn out that way at all. In fact, I still remember my son saying sometime during those difficult days that this was the best Christmas ever. I had to agree. Lying in bed during my recuperation, I had plenty of time to think and I came to understand that our circumstances could have been worse. God had spared my life, and I was convinced that God had more for me to do.

The court detective assigned to my case had discovered that the man who ran me over fled the scene because he had no insurance.

***

I was eventually back on my feet. Although I was never fully healed from the accident, I woke each morning with the understanding that as long as the Spirit of God was with me, I would make it. One morning the alarm sounded, but before rolling out of bed, I took an extra five minutes just to think through the rest of my day. The children were doing very well in their respective schools. I was adjusting at work with my new responsibilities. My family in Barbados, England, Canada and Maryland were also doing well. We honestly were at a good place in our life. Life had finally become less precarious, and in faith we had a good future to look forward to.

On that encouraging thought, I sat up in my bed and swung my legs over the side, ready to get started on my day. But at my first step, I collapsed back onto the bed. I was unable to feel my lower legs! It was as if they were made of rubber. I tried consciously to move just my feet and realized I could not feel my toes. The realization hit me that I was unable to stand up on my own. I was immediately filled with fear. It came on so fast, I couldn't stop myself from screaming out. My scream echoed throughout the house, and soon my children were running into my room. Calmer now, I told them to go to school and that God would take care of me. But my youngest daughter Crystal was holding me and crying, refusing to let go, telling me that I was going to be okay. While my middle daughter looked after getting Junie off to school, my oldest daughter Barbara massaged my calves and feet until gradually the blood began to flow back into them. I regained feeling.

Although I was feeling a little better, I decided to go to the doctor. I called out of work, praying that I would hear the magic words "You are going to be all right." A church neighbor drove me to the doctor's office. After removing my shoes, I noticed that the floor was cold and that the walls were a dreary gray color, a perfect accompaniment to how I was feeling. The nurse performed the usual series of small tests every newly arrived patient is given. Before the doctor arrived, it was enlightening to hear from the nurse that Dr. Ally was considered one of the best doctors in our neighborhood. She assured me he was very good with arthritic patients and that I had nothing to worry about.

But her very words flooded my thoughts with new concern. Arthritis? I hadn't even thought about such a thing! Was that my problem? Immediately I thought of my mother, crippled while still quite young, and my heart began to pound with worry.

When the doctor came in, his piercing light brown eyes stared straight into mine from behind glasses that closely nuzzled the bridge of his nose. I extended my hand to greet him, but he simply nodded, hardly noticing. Apparently, he was too intent on reviewing my chart and what he had to say to worry about niceties. After his complete examination, the doctor got straight to the point.

"You have rheumatoid arthritis, which is the severest of cases and unfortunately incurable."

"What? What is this disease? I have never heard of such a thing."

"Rheumatoid arthritis is an autoimmune disease that can cause chronic inflammation of the joints and other areas of the body. That is why you were unable to stand up properly this morning. Look at your hands. Do you see how the joints are red, flared and tender? That is the first clear sign. Based on the other results from the blood test, it does not look good."

"My mother had the very symptoms you've mentioned, we just weren't aware of the name for the disease. Surely there are medicines or treatments for this?"

He was blunt and to the point. "I am sorry, Mrs. Matias. Right now there is no known cure for this disease. You can take ibuprofen on days when the pain is light, but I will also prescribe a stronger medicine for days when the pain is unbearable. As the disease increases, you will have days when you feel fatigued, with lack of appetite, low fever, muscle and joint aches along with stiffness within the body. Your muscles will feel most painful in the morning."

"What does this all mean? I have children to take care of. I'm a supervisor at the Met requiring a four hour a day commute — and how will inflamed joints effect my use of a calculator for accounting work. What am I going to do?"

"I am really sorry," the doctor told me. "I wish I could tell you something different. Simple tasks of daily living, such as writing a letter, turning doorknobs, brushing your teeth and opening jars will become difficult. Sometimes the arthritis will even affect the joint that is responsible for the tightening of your vocal cords. Your voice may change, lower in tone. You may experience hoarseness and even, in some cases, the loss of your voice. There is nothing more I can do."

Dr. Ally left the room without saying another word, leaving me with my thoughts. I sat in the silent room, and I turned to memories of my mother, who had spent her last days on this earth in severe pain. Unable to help with the raising of her children or the running of her household, she had lived like a prisoner in her own castle. I recalled the many days she had sat and wept because her pain was so great. And now I was facing much the same future.

Why, God? Why me? I prayed. *I have done my best. I have remained faithful to you. A life sentence of pain and deformity? What about the many nights I stayed up late to read my Bible and prayed? What about the sacrifices I have made for my family? Can you hear me, God? Are you listening? God, this is just not right! This is not fair! I cannot take it anymore. God, you have said you are a healer. If so, then heal me. Take away this pain, oh God, please take away this pain!*

I sat unmoving on the examination table, unwilling to get up to leave – as if the very act of leaving the doctor's office with this new knowledge would make it real and irrevocable. I continued to sit there, tears streaming down my face at the realization that our life was going to change yet again. But what could I do except keep moving forward and do my best to adjust to this new challenge?

I pulled myself together and thought about how much my children still needed me. For their sake, I could not give up. *God*, I prayed again, *please give me the strength to make it through this next challenge in my life.* Like Job's portrayal of faith in action in the Old Testament, I too said, "Though God slay me, yet will I serve him."

After getting my prescriptions filled, I went home in a taxi and started trying to deal with my new normal life. I contacted my employer with my medical update and advised them of who from the staff should cover my position until I returned from a short leave of absence.

CHAPTER 16

The Privilege of Parenting

I was young and now I am old,
yet I have never seen the righteous forsaken
or their children begging bread.
They are always generous and lend freely;
their children will be a blessing.

—Psalm 37:25–26

My parents instilled in me the ambition to achieve the highest level of education I possibly could. Likewise, Benton and I had agreed when our children were very young that they must go to college. When they were of college age, it seemed an impossible goal on a single parent's income.

Barbara wanted to go away from home to attend a school which was a plane flight away. Even though the institution was a Christian university, I felt initial hesitation over her being so far away from home. However, with God's favor and with the assured confidence of a bright student, she packed her bags. The day before she left, I fixed a kind of goodbye dinner for all of us, and she and I seemed to share a special bond that evening, laughing and talking. I was proud of all that my daughter had accomplished up until then and was certain that great opportunities were yet to come.

At the airport the next day, I couldn't help remembering when my brother Vincent had gone off to England all those years ago, and I felt a sudden emptiness. Barbara was off to a new city and might never return to Brooklyn to live. But I knew that I had to let her go. She is a wonderful daughter and a wonderful young woman who believes in Christian values. She had never given me a difficult moment. She knew right from wrong, and she knew how to take care of herself. If anyone was going to be all right on her own, it was Barbara. So I put my trust in God that He would keep her safe.

"Remember to call me when you arrive," I reminded her. "I love you." With tears welling up in my eyes, I gave her one last hug.

Then, with strong wings she soared through the gateway towards the plane and out of sight.

A mere one year later, I found myself preparing for my second daughter to leave for college. Chelsie had decided to attend a college located just six hours away. On the day she left, Chelsie piled her boxes and suitcases into the van of a church friend. In the warm, morning air, surrounded by the bluest of skies, we happily welcomed this Saturday drive to get Chelsie settled into her dorm. As we drove around the campus, I could sense Chelsie's excitement at starting a new life in such a new and interesting setting. I was almost as excited as she was and happy she would be close enough to come home more frequently than her sister could. After Chelsie settled into her dorm, we shared, a long warm hug. While Chelsie was saying goodbye to her friends, I thought about how she had told me that someday she would buy a house where she and I would live together and where she would take care of me. Chelsie's ambition was such that I couldn't help but to look forward with wonderful expectations to how the next steps in her life would work out.

Crystal's commute to college was less than five hours away. I was really happy as all three of the girls were in college. I could hardly believe it – except when the bills came. Benton never contributed to their spending money, books, tuition nor room and board, so I did the best I could and when I could do no more, I believe that in God's sovereignty, He stepped in. I believe He is the bond in my family relationships; I believe He provided money and resources through unexpected channels and in the ninth hour when I least expected it.

The girls came home for the Christmas holiday to celebrate the season and Crystal's and my birthday. During this visit, they updated me with all their school news and changes in their social lives. I was pleased to know that they were all doing very well academically, spiritually and socially.

The years passed as if they were months, and before I knew it, I was on my way to college graduations. I was a proud parent and enjoyed experiencing American university graduations for the first time. Where had the years gone? Only the grace of God could have made the impossible, possible! Somehow God's favor seemed to step in right on time. I was living vicariously through my daughters.

Soon after their graduations, my daughters were arranging to marry boyfriends they'd met in college. Their boyfriends each respectively took the proper traditional steps by asking for my daughters' hands in marriage. I was overjoyed to give my permission. It was an exciting time as each of their weddings took place just steps apart as they were all three married over the course of a few years. I was ecstatically beside myself with elation. I could foresee the family expanding into soft little hands and feet and bright innocent smiles and hugs. I would have the honor to be called Grandmommy. The wedding plans all got off to a good start for each occasion respectively. Not surprisingly, however, when it came time for the wedding planning, Benton announced that he hadn't any money to contribute to the occasion, so I would need to find a way to help pay for these weddings. I didn't let this circumstance get me down. I took care of what I could, such as the flower and photo packages and the reception expenses for a few of my colleagues and church friends that just had to be there. For years, I had put my trust in God to make up the difference. He always has.

They made handsome grooms and beautiful brides. Months of preparation, phone calls to florists, catering halls, photographers and limo companies exhaust any loving parent. Through it all, the family needed to remain patient in the process – it is during late hours of deliberation that relationships are tried to the last bone. Fortunately, the love and support of family and friends kept us together.

The wedding ceremonies and receptions for all three of my daughters were well attended. There were now three couples who needed to come together to learn from each other, with hopes of growing old together. There are always obstacles to overcome. The trick I've learned and my children lived through is that both parties in the marriage need to love God, love each other, stick together and overcome together.

Benton and I both loved the Lord and still our marriage had not worked. I have never understood how Benton could have made the immoral choices he made – to break so many commandments, particularly the one not to commit adultery – and still claim to love and honor the Lord. But it wasn't my place to judge. Through untiring faith in God's sovereign guidance and divine purpose, I understood that God's grace is sufficient. I stood strong in the Lord and the power of his might. What I learned is that when the storms of life relentlessly barrel down, my Christian beliefs give me hope for tomorrow. I took super sour lemons and made sweet, refreshing, thirst-quenching lemonade. Then I rested in the peace of God that passes all understanding that guards my heart and mind through Christ Jesus.

I am so pleased to have an awareness of the power of peace that comes from faith in God. I am grateful to have had many a happy holiday and special occasions with my daughters and their families. This happy ending to child rearing has gone a long way to replace many uncontrollable disappointments.

Thank you, God, for family and for Your amazing grace!

CHAPTER 17

From Death to Life

"Where, O death, is your victory? Where, O death, is your sting?"
The sting of death is sin, and the power of sin is the law.
But thanks be to God!
He gives us the victory through our Lord Jesus Christ.

—1 Corinthians 15:55–57

The sound of a telephone off hours tends to cause my heart to skip a beat. One evening in November 1990, when the sound of a ringing phone jolted me out of a deep sleep at 2 a.m., it didn't occur to me to hesitate. I picked up the phone and said hello – to a mother's worst nightmare. It was my youngest daughter Crystal. She asked me to get ready and said that we would have to go to Brooklyn right away. My heart instinctively began racing as fast as a runaway train with a derailed destination when she announced that Junie had been in an accident.

Clumsily, I returned the phone to its cradle. *This has to be a dream*, I thought. But of course it wasn't. As I dressed as quickly as I possibly could, I glanced toward the picture of Junie escorting me down the aisle at Chelsie's wedding. I started praying and asked God what was going on. I immediately decided to trust the Lord in all things like I'd done many times before. I thought more about the conversation with Crystal. An accident, she'd said. Was Junie driving? Did he get hit by another car? Or was a car involved at all?

Sometime after, the lights of the car blazed like a star amidst the absence of sunlight outside my Edison, New Jersey apartment. I put on my coat, locked my door, and proceeded to the car, wondering what to say and what to ask. After warm greetings in the car, no one seemed inclined to talk. It was as if we were all in the same boat as to what was going on. What I did know was that whatever had happened, it had taken place in Brooklyn. While en route to the scene of the crime, the city streets of Brooklyn appeared surprisingly abandoned. What had happened to the city that never sleeps that was once my residence? An eerie fog seeped through the tall apartment buildings onto the street. The mist and the silence were almost hypnotizing, and I became lost in my thoughts. Soon we arrived at the familiar street where members of my previous church family still lived. It had been at least a year since I had visited my previous neighborhood that held such fond memories, but given the current situation, it felt very different to be back. Stepping out of the car, I asked myself, *Why are we here?* I was confused, because I was expecting that we were going to the hospital.

As I walked through the gate of the sidewalk entrance stairs, I could see that the lights in the basement, first and second floors were curiously all on at this time of night. I walked slowly up another set of orange brick colored steps to the front door. We rang the doorbell. Immediately the door swung open as if my daughter's mother-in-law had been standing in the foyer entrance patiently awaiting our arrival. She reached out to hug me and straightaway lavished me with words of sympathy. Maybe she thought I knew what had happened. It was obvious to me at that moment that she knew. I was now in a colossally elevated level of dread. I could almost hear my heart palpitating. I pleaded for someone to tell me where Junie was, what hospital he was in. As we walked past the foyer toward the living room, she talked about something to do with the Thanksgiving season being the worst time to bring this type of news. I could sense that the others knew details about Junie's accident that they hadn't told me and were beating around the bush trying to find the right words. I could not take the anticipation anymore when I heard someone say,

"Junie is dead. He has been shot."

"No!" I screamed in anguished disbelief.

I immediately became tense and my heart raced out of control. I could feel my blood pressure raise so high that if I did not release steam I would explode. I started pacing and sobbing profusely and just when I was overcome with weakness, Crystal hugged me and guided me to the living room area's couch.

I looked in Crystal's bloodshot weeping eyes and said, "Tell me this is not true."

Without an uttered word, we fell into one another's arms and in mutual empathy embraced each other, holding on tightly as if that embrace were our last lifeline. I shook all over. My only son – gone? How? Why? I silently prayed to God for strength and frantically cried out to God. I was hysterically brokenhearted like never before.

My daughter's mother-in-law sat on the other side of me and placed her hand ever so sympathetically on my back. I turned to her and from one mother to another I cried on her shoulder. I could not understand why God would allow this to happen. There was no time or space to understand. It was not fair. Junie had just turned 20 years old in August. In shock, my mind's eye drifted to the last time I saw him towering over me at 6 feet tall and I thought about how he was such a handsome young man with his light Indian skin tone, black curly hair, bright green eyes and an amazing smile that always warmed my heart. Suddenly, my aching eyes released a bucket of heartfelt tears which poured down my cheeks. I was smitten in utter disbelief. It took several hours to catch my breath. I prayed, *God I love you and worship you but this is all too sudden: my heart is gravely heavy. I can't bear this heavy cross alone.* I thought that Junie was to become a preacher and take over where his father had left off. He was trustworthy and an overall respectful young man and I had experienced his caring heart firsthand.

I was handed a glass of water and a roll of toilet paper as together all weeping eyes had used up the box of tissues.

When Junie's best friend arrived to the house, he explained to me the details of what happened earlier that night.

Junie was around the corner and standing outside of the 24-hour grocery store on Church Avenue. He was talking to his girlfriend when a car pulled up and began shooting. With witness from the store attendant and girlfriend, I learned that Junie initially jumped in front of his girlfriend to protect her, then ran as if to cause a chase away from the young lady. This heroic act ended fatally as he was murdered by several gunshots in the back. Then the drive-by shooters sped away, and there Junie lay on the ground as the blood was flowing out of his body taking along with it his last breath. I didn't know this girlfriend, but I could only imagine then that his girlfriend grabbed him and held him as if it would somehow bring him back, but it was too late. He had passed on.

After thanking Junie's friend for sharing the details around the murder, I was able to gather myself just enough to talk with a quiver to my voice. I explained that Junie was supposed to come to New Jersey last night but he had decided to stay with his friends. I regret now that I hadn't insisted that he come home as planned.

I could not go to identify the body. I just couldn't face the reality of Junie's death. I wanted it to be a bad nightmare from which I would eventually awake. Junie had grown into the man who would keep me safe – so different from Daddy or Benton Sr. Junie had loved and protected me as the man of the house. I couldn't bear to think he was gone.

A few young men from the Nazarene church went to the morgue and confirmed that it was indeed Junie. When they returned, all we could do was weep together. At the door of age twenty years old, Junie's life was over. I went berserk and began beating on everyone closest to me, until my daughter's father-in-law, who was a nurse, took my blood pressure and announced that I needed to go directly to the hospital, and there I went.

***

The day of Junie's funeral, my reflections were filled with grief. I thought, *God, You promised me in my prayers that Junie would preach and many would be saved.* The evening of Junie's funeral service is still a bit of a blur to me. I remember riding to the church in a black limousine. While sitting in the car, I looked down at my hand and remembered that one of the stones from my gold ring was missing. This was a special ring that I wore every day after receiving it from my children during the previous Christmas. It had four stones in the ring that represented the birth months of my children. I was absolutely surprised at the irony: the one stone related to Junie's birthday was the only one that had gone mysteriously missing. I remembered that a week prior to the dreadfully alarming something-is-wrong phone call that the stone representing Junie's birthday fell out and I was planning to have it replaced the following weekend. Had this been a message from God preparing me that my son would be gone only a week later?

On arrival at the church, we were led to the front of the sanctuary by ushers dressed in white who seated us with the rest of the family. As I glanced around, a sea of black suits and dresses and hats adorned the family and friends who came to pay their respects and show their support.

As I sat waiting for the start of the service, I had a calming memory. The morning of Junie's death, I had spoken to him on the telephone. He had respectfully called to say, amongst other things, that he would not be home that night. He also took the time to express how much he loved me and the Lord. He encouraged me not to worry about him and said, "Mommy, I love you and I talk to God everyday as clearly as I am talking to you, so don't worry." Those words got me through the saddest, most comprehensive grief I'd ever encountered at that time. As a result, I was convinced that I would see Junie someday in heaven.

There were such an influx of guests with close friends greeting me with hugs and words of comfort. Some, not knowing what to say, just hugged me and walked away. Even the young friends from the community that Junie had held so dear came and gave me a hug with tears in their eyes. The organist filled the sanctuary with somber but peaceful hymns. I thought about how I had sat in the same seat of the same pew several times with tears of joy in my eyes as my daughters said their wedding vows. But this evening, I sat with tears of despair.

The casket – a cold, steel cocoon that encased the body of my only son – was only a few feet away. Barely able to function, I held tightly to my daughters Barbara, Chelsie and Crystal for support.

The pastor began the service with a prayer and offered up a few words of comfort to the friends and family. His choice of biblical reference was appropriate for the occasion:

> *Brothers and sisters, we do not want you to be uninformed about those who sleep in death, so that you do not grieve like the rest of mankind, who have no hope. For we believe that Jesus died and rose again, and so we believe that God will bring with Jesus those who have fallen asleep in him. According to the Lord's word, we tell you that we who are still alive, who are left until the coming of the Lord, will certainly not precede those who have fallen asleep. For the Lord himself will come down from heaven, with a loud command, with the voice of the archangel and with the trumpet call of God, and the dead in Christ will rise first. After that, we who are still alive and are left will be caught up together with them in the clouds to meet the Lord in the air. And so we will be with the Lord forever. Therefore encourage one another with these words.*

–1 Thessalonians 4:13–18

The pastor continued with what was apparently his prepared sermon, but he suddenly stopped and looked into the congregation. He had known my family for many years. He had seen my son grow up from a little boy to an aspiring, young, handsome, and promising young man. Now, when he spoke again, he left his prepared speech behind. Instead, he poured his heart out in pain over the needless, tragic loss of Junie's life. He pleaded to all with an outreach to the teenagers present to remember that none of us know the last day or hour that we will live.

"Give your heart to Jesus tonight," he urged. "Do not delay, for tomorrow is not promised to anyone."

He continued to speak with tears rolling down his cheek. Finally, he offered a prayer of hope and condolence for the family. Then he introduced my daughter Crystal, who shared a melody that was Junie's favorite Christian song.

We all held our breath, uncertain whether she would make it through the song without breaking down. The room was quiet and still as the keyboard player began to play the introduction. Crystal stood straight and square, holding on to the podium. Then, taking the microphone in her hand, and with sincerity of conviction she deeply sang out the song, "Tomorrow," by BeBe Winans, beckoning all to receive God's love and forgiveness that day because tomorrow is not promised to anybody.

I had an epiphany when I noticed the way the church was packed. There were hundreds and hundreds of people, a crowd like those that came during special services such as Easter and Christmas programs. Tonight, there was not an empty seat in the sanctuary and it soon became clear that God was causing something special, something promised to happen in the midst of our pain. It was a blessing that many young people showed up to express their sympathy and were scattered throughout the lower sanctuary pews and balcony, with only standing room remaining.

At the end of the rendition of the song "Tomorrow," like Easter, the funeral service brought awareness of the love of God in an amazingly tangible way. After the call for prayer, one by one, a countless amount of attendees young and old swamped the altar and surrounded the casket where Junie laid. With open hearts, people pressed their way to receive God's love and forgiveness, burying their faces in their hands as they walked. Weeping, they united in faith at the altar.

Even in my pain, I suddenly understood God's plan – Junie's life was an instrument to bring many new souls to the awareness of the Lord's unfailing love for mankind. Among the youth were people who probably would not have ever attended regular church services, but here they were at Junie's funeral service, opening their hearts to Christ by simply choosing to believe that *"God so loved the world that he gave his one and only son that whoever believes in him shall not perish but have eternal life"* (John 3:16).

The pain I felt for the death of my son was soothed a bit as I saw God's promise to use Junie to save many people from their sins come true right before my eyes. With a sharpened sense of faith, I watched mothers and fathers from the church family join in to hug and pray with the many people who now surrounded the casket at the front of the church.

That moment is what I remember the most about that day, and because of it, I felt a sense of resolve instead of just dismay. Silently, I bid my son goodbye. I had been proud of his authentic love for God, family and community during the prime of his life. I will miss him.

***

The interment was held the next morning, for immediate family only. We gathered at the graveside and held hands as the pastor prayed. Then we each had an opportunity to make a final statement. We all held different colored carnations selected from the arrangement that draped the casket. With our final comments, we tossed our flowers onto the casket. It was Benton Senior's turn to speak.

With dark shades covering his red, bloodshot eyes, he said, "Junie, I am so sorry, my son. I have failed you as a father. You needed me, and I was not there for you. This is my entire fault. Please forgive me, Junie. I am so sorry." He then wailed, "Why, God, did you take my only son? God, take me instead, take me."

In that solemn heart-heavy moment, Benton stepped forward as if to leap into the grave, but thank God one of my son-in-law's had bullseye sharp reflexes and reached forward and pulled Benton back, holding him from falling into the grave. As I watched this scene that appeared to happen faster than the speed of light, Benton cried, something I rarely saw him do. In that disenchanting moment, he must finally have realized what he had done and all he had lost by not taking part in his children's lives. There was nothing more to say.

***

After an extended amount of time of living through the grieving process, in quiet times I had fond memories of Junie and I wept. It was hard as it was the first time I was living alone. But God was with me and through a routine of keeping in touch with my daughters and my church family, prayer and reading the word of God before traveling to work daily, the peace of God helped me to bear the sorrow that accompanies the passing of a loved one. Although no one could ever fill the shoes of an only son gone to heaven, the good news that my eldest daughter started a family brought jubilant thoughts of being a grandparent. The imagery of my grandson's pattering little feet brought an outlandish smile to my heart and a hopeful outlook for the family's future.

When I returned to work, my colleagues and friends showered me with heartfelt sympathy cards and tried to help me take my mind off things by frequently asking which one of my children would be the next to give birth to a grandchild.

My oldest daughter's son sent waves of joy throughout the family. I could see God completing another one of His promises. He was expanding my family. I called often to check on Barbara, to make sure she was resting properly. As the proud grandmother, I scheduled a plane trip to help her care for the bouncing baby boy. I could see the DNA mix from both family lines. As I held him he seemed to have a little smile of hello for his grandma.

I had planned to spend the week in order to give Barbara a hand so she could rest. To my surprise, she was up the next day in the kitchen preparing breakfast for me.

"Barbara, come sit down and let me do that for you. I came here to give you a helping hand."

"I know, but I need to move. I will need your help more, later, when the baby wakes up."

Just then, the soft movement in the basinet put a pep in my step and I stood to attend the waking prince. His eyes widened when I greeted him with a "Good morning, your grandma is here." Then I sang a familiar church tune that talks about waking and shining and giving God the glory. I smiled with him and he smiled back at me as if he recognized a familiar voice. I scooped him up and walked towards the living room where a comfortable couch was waiting for the both of us to continue enjoying our bonding moments.

The role of motherhood suited Barbara. She would laugh and play with her new little one as often as possible. At the end of my visit, I was certain she was going to be a capable and loving mother. On the flight back to New Jersey, I thought about how proud I was of her. I just had to tell the person sitting next to me on the plane all about my experiences. I was a brand new grandmother! And I was so happy that the next generation had begun. Like the domino effect, the grandchildren's birthdates would come to remind me of my mother's childbearing days, but instead of siblings every year, I would help take care of my grandchildren. That was a miraculous conclusion to thank God for.

As soon as my Edison, New Jersey apartment lease was up, I decided to start a new chapter in my life's timeline in Sayreville, New Jersey. I moved to a first floor, one bedroom apartment near my youngest daughter, Crystal. Although in those days most people retired when they turned 65, this early retirement of mine would take place in my early 50s. I chose to retire from the Metropolitan Museum of Art due not to personal desire or company demand but in line with the unfortunate impediment of the slowly crippling rheumatoid arthritis that plagued my joints and undermined an already daunting five-hour roundtrip commute from Edison, New Jersey to Queens, New York. After positively fulfilling twenty-plus years of commitment, it was a sad last day when I gathered the personal items I had accumulated at the Met. I carefully wrapped all the pictures of my children and the parting gifts from my co-workers, and placed them in appropriately-sized packing containers. There were several beautiful paintings from the Met that I still keep in my home as memories of my most wonderful job and my faithful coworkers, who generously threw a delightful retirement party as my big send off.

***

Retirement! I couldn't begin to imagine what this would mean to me, a woman who had worked for the majority of her life. But I was determined that this was not going to be the end of my productive years. I had always loved children so I would babysit my grandchildren during the day. And perhaps I could become more involved with the church, as I used to be in Barbados and Brooklyn. With those few thoughts, I began to smile. Making new plans was helping to lift my spirits. There were things I could still do, after all. I was determined that this was not an end to the best part of my life but rather, like it was for Christopher Columbus, it was the beginning of a future with unchartered waters yet to be discovered.

As I lived near my daughter Crystal, I would make dinner every work night as she traveled to New York City for employment. I would cook a delicious meal made up of a combination of American and Barbadian cuisines. They were well-balanced with a meat, chicken or fish, a carbohydrate and vegetables. I made enough to feed any of my family members that would stop by for dinner, as Chelsie's family lived just about 25 minutes away.

One evening set a new precedent in my relationship and connection with Crystal. I remember it like it was just yesterday. I was preparing a main dish of curry chicken stew made with potatoes, which I would pick out before consuming, due to their ability to cause an arthritic flare up. That evening, dinner was accompanied by a blend of green pigeon peas and rice, boiled together until tender, and a medley of steamed broccoli, cauliflower and butternut squash. I left cooking the vegetables for a time close to when Crystal would arrive from off the Academy bus so they would be nice and fresh without being reheated.

During the day I would clean and challenge myself to a variety of crossword puzzle topics, write in my journal, and read the latest health magazine. I'd spend quality quiet time that included the worship of God, the reading of Bible scriptures, prayer for my family and friends and often for God's perfect will to be done, as noted in the popular Lord's prayer: *"Our Father in heaven, hallowed be your name, your kingdom come, your will be done, on earth as it is in heaven. Give us today our daily bread. And forgive us our debts, as we also have forgiven our debtors. And lead us not into temptation, but deliver us from the evil one"* (Matthew 6:9–13). The living room was located just off the main entrance and positioned directly in front of the kitchen, which was separated off by a wall. The dining room was to the left of the kitchen and viewable from the living room. The dining room table was the only place to sit down to have a formal meal. It was decorated with a lace tablecloth and a spring-colored floral centerpiece.

After she knocked at the door, Crystal and I greeted each other with a hug and kiss right before I began to internally gloat from her high praises of how wonderfully dinner smelled. She offered to help, but I insisted that she take a load off while I put on the vegetables to steam and set the dinner table. Unbeknownst to me, Crystal stumbled across my journal that I kept tucked away in the living room near my reading materials.

After reading quite a bit, she came across a part of my history that she had not known and was brought to tears to read that I was taken advantage of by my father. Right there and then she approached me in a desperate disbelief.

"Mommy what is this book?"

I stopped what I was doing when I noticed Crystal was upset.

"It's my journal. Why are you crying? Are you O.K.?"

"Don't worry, I'll be fine, but I was just reading your journal and am familiar with most of it until I get to the part about how you were taken advantage of by Granddaddy, that makes me so very upset! I can't believe this!"

I tried to comfort her. "Crystal, don't cry. It was a long time ago and I have forgiven him."

She continued, "That is totally sick! If you can't trust your own father, who can you trust?"

"I did trust him."

I reached out to her and we held each other in what I felt was the warmest, most compassionate embrace we had ever shared.

"Initially it did not strike me as a private journal as the content was so familiar until that one point about you and Granddaddy. I'm sorry."

"Oh please, sweetie, sorry for what? What's mine is yours. I'm just sorry it upset you so much."

I handed her tissue to dry her tears.

As I made a salad, I handed the salad bowl and dressing to Crystal to put on the table. To help soothe the sting of the revelation, I suggested that we eat. After blessing the food, it was our family practice to be thankful to God for His provisions before eating.

In no time, Crystal continued the conversation about what Daddy had done.

"I'm amazed that your life does not resemble what you went through. If it were me, I would have gone bonkers. You endured so much trauma but yet you are such an angel. If I did not read this myself, I would have never known. You do not look or sound like what you've gone through. Mom, if I never told you this before, I admire everything about you. You lead with such a level of courage. You lead by example leaving no stone unturned. You give everyone around you a sense that you have thought of everything. Your love for people and your faith in God is so consistent that I can truly say that I've not come across many people like you. Simply stated, you don't miss a beat. I wish I could be more like you in so many ways."

I was touched by her loving adoration. Without hesitation I shared that God's amazing grace is sufficient for me and can be for anyone that puts faith in God.

"Mom I'm taken by how your life has been such a challenge, yet you have this peace about you that is so genuine."

"Crystal dear, the truth of the matter is that I gave my heart to the Lord. And He has made a world of the difference."

After dinner we cleared the plates from the table and jovially tussled over who would wash the dishes. In an attempt to bring a smile to Crystal's face, I assured her that she was on the right track and that she is a chip off the old block. Needless to say, I lost the coin toss and Crystal did the dishes.

After she returned to her home and I was doing my nightly prayers for the family before bedtime, my memory kicked in about Crystal. I thought about our special time together that day and about how she was born on my Christmas birthday. We were clearly developing a deeper bond. That all transitioned into an individual prayer where I knew that God would bless whatever she'd put her hands to do.

In Jesus's name, I closed my eyes to rest.

**

After living in the Sayreville, New Jersey neighborhood, I was invited to move into my daughter Chelsie's home where her husband had completely finished their walkout basement and converted it into a one-bedroom apartment just for me. With its family room designed as a play area for the grandchildren, the layout was more spacious than my Sayreville home. It had an eat-in kitchen, living and dining room that boasted windows and a glass sliding door that brought in a large amount of sunlit rays that penetrated through the tree-lined view and rested on a nicely manicured, evenly green, grass-covered backyard. This living arrangement was a win-win situation. I treasured the time helping to raise the grandchildren, cooking and sharing holidays with family. I really appreciated the family driving me to church and my doctor appointments. I was no longer living alone.

To my utter delight, in the early 1990s Crystal's family had moved from Sayreville into their new home also. One day, she came to visit me to reveal a truly amazing opportunity that was recently proposed to her. Beaming from ear to ear, she asked me to sit down on the same couch where she had first read my journal entries. At this point, I was getting excited myself and was more than happy to take a seat. As Crystal was pacing, I was more settled when she joined me on my comfy couch. The good news was around receiving a visit from two well-groomed, middle-aged Caucasian men from the New York area, who were dressed casually in jeans and colored shirts. In the past, these gentlemen had brought in the musical *Gee, Whiz God Is* that Crystal had co-written, directed and produced. They were looking to work together with Crystal's team to bring in another show. She went on with a heightened level of enthusiasm to express that during this informal meeting she didn't have a finished script available to be produced but that what she did have was an idea for a script that would be based on a true story about a woman, who in spite of her trials and tragedies in life, didn't give up on her faith in God. With expediency, they articulated that they loved the idea and said, "Let's do it," as it was the type of thing they were looking for.

Then Crystal turned to me with a massive measure of passion, ready to erupt at any moment, and asked me, "Do you know who that woman of faith is?"

I sat there still as a deer stunned by a car's headlights, not sure if she expected me to answer, or if it was a rhetorical question, or if I should just wait for her to spill it out.

Crystal exploded with elated glee, "It's your life story!" She refreshed my memory about our previous conversation around the direct impact I've had on her life.

Without hesitation, cheerful words of encouragement flowed from my lips to her ears, "Crystal, that's just wonderful, God surely is working in your favor in mysterious ways! You've done it before, so I know you can do it again."

With further conversation around the sensitivity of the story, there was an initial concern around privacy. We went on to focus on the positive influence my life of faith could have on other people, just as it had had on her.

"Mom, your life blessed my socks off so I know it will bless others. Besides, it's not just about me. Why do you think everyone calls you Mommy Matias? It's a term of endearment used by your friends and members of your church community for a reason. All the youth at the church as well as the adults love you. How about the people you supervised and your manager? They all have expressed their appreciation and demonstrated their respect for you down through the years as they viewed your character in action. After all you've gone through, you are breathing a victorious life. People that know you might see your current story as regular, but they don't know your journey of trusting in God's promises that undergirds the drive behind your life of faith."

After some thought about my testimony being a blessing to others, I conceded. Having adopted Jesus's teachings around love, forgiveness and faith in God into my daily life, it has brought liberty to my soul and a peace of mind to my existence. And to have the opportunity to share my story with others, at a chance that someone would experience renewed hope, is what loving your neighbor is all about. I believe what the Bible proclaims when it talks about God being no respecter of persons. He opens up His loving promises to everyone who would believe.

Crystal receiving my agreement to move forward with the musical launched my relationship with her into a new direction that had everything to do with being active examples of lives of faith well-lived. Glory to God!

CHAPTER 18

Back to Barbados

For by me your days will be multiplied,
And years of life will be added to you.

—Proverbs 9:11 (NKJV)

Winter 1995 found me in Barbados with my family, celebrating the landmark age of sixty. Remembering that my mother died in her early 60s, I prayed and asked God for at least 15 more years of life. After that I was ready to enjoy the merriments. I was glad that at this junction of my journey, my caring, giving family held my birthday festivities on our beautiful island. As I walked along the beach at the resort where we all stayed, I reflected on the path that God had led me along thus far. It had been a long, lonely journey sometimes, but there had been unexpected friends at each turn of the path and angels guarding and keeping me from dangers seen and unseen. Despite my human frailty, God had kept me strong through all the events of my life. I thank Him, now, that He shielded my family and me so well. Despite disappointments and tragedy, God faithfully continued to lift me and mine above it all, to face another day and to count our blessings.

I have to admit, my journey as a Christian has proven to help make life worth the living. When I was running as fast as I could and soaring through the winds as a school-aged child, I didn't know then that I would be a devoted Christian today, but I am so very glad I am. I have occasionally met exciting and interesting people in my life, but most important of all to me is having a family that loves and cares for me and I them. I raised my children with unconditional love and it continues to flow from heart to heart. I was honored that everyone had come together for a family reunion in celebration of my sixtieth birthday.

The resort where we stayed was near the parish of St. Michael. Inside was an elegant and spacious restaurant that offered marvelous views of the sea and sky and ample seating for the many invited friends and family. Invitations had been sent out three months in advance to allow time for all the out-of-town guests to confirm their attendance. I was elated by the overwhelming positive response. Many had written that they would not miss this birthday celebration for anything in the world, including my then ex-husband's dear sister and her family.

My sister Faith coordinated all the food and entertainment for the party. She decided that instead of cooking for this special event, she would hire a caterer so that she could enjoy the celebration, too. Balloons and other decorations adorned the entire restaurant, and soulful Caribbean beats underscored all the activities of the day. Faith hired a local disc jockey to play some of the older and more familiar tunes from my time.

My other sister Yasmin, a talented hairstylist on the island, came by my hotel room early that day to style my hair for this special occasion. She also took the time to apply my makeup and do my nails. Wow! I felt like I was in a day spa! I had wanted to wear something bright and festive for the occasion, so my son-in-law had designed a beautiful beaded jacket and matching dress just for this special event. With matching shoes and a sparkling clutch bag I purchased earlier that week, I was extra enthusiastic.

When it was time for the grand ballroom entrance, I was escorted to a special table by my older brother Vincent who had flown in from England. In addition to enjoying the gorgeous, bountiful bouquet of flowers at the head table, I was elated to be positioned in a seat where I could see each guest arrive. It was difficult for me to stay seated as I wanted to run up and greet each personally, but my brother reminded me that I needed to stay in place and let the guests come to me. Vincent announced that the family intended to treat me like royalty and that all I needed would be served to me. "If there is anything you would like, just let me know." I had never been treated with such tender, loving care during a birthday party in Barbados. Everyone was dripping with honey and I graciously lapped it up!

On nearby tables were displayed all my favorite foods, including items I couldn't get back home in America like flying fish and breadfruit. At another table, desserts were beautifully displayed, along with my birthday cake. For those who enjoyed spirits, my brother Leon provided the open bar, but included refreshing coconut water and the Juicy and Fruity brand soft drinks for me and the attending children. It was a heartwarming, memorable evening for me. All night long, my family teased me, saying "Queen Margaret is here." As Barbados is a commonwealth of Great Brittan, being called a queen, even in jest, had great significance. I felt so appreciated and honored!

I was sure to take a few moments to thank God for His way of balancing the stings of life with these moments of happiness. The celebration went on late into the night. I specifically marveled at the delightful time my brothers and sisters were having, liming (bonding in a relaxing atmosphere), laughing and singing familiar songs. My siblings and young adult children enjoyed themselves in Calypso style, creating a "jump-up" environment on the dance floor. It was such a pleasure to see everyone enjoying life and having a memorable time. When they were done dancing, everyone was truly feeling "Hot, Hot, Hot."

Love is something you cannot buy, nor put a price on, so I just sat back smiled and thanked God for this special time, not knowing when I would be able to visit this beautiful Island of Barbados again.

***

The next day I was awakened by the bright sun peeping into my room. I arose quickly and smiled when I saw the gifts and cards scattered about my room, all happy reminders of my birthday party the night before. But just as precious to me were thoughts of the many wonderful Barbadians who had come not necessarily bearing gifts but most importantly bringing their love and their desire to see me. With utter wonder, I deeply thought about the family members who had flown in from Canada, England and the United States especially to attend the party. I knew the trip and festivities were a sacrifice for some of them, and I really appreciated every last bit of the entire occasion.

The resort provided a wonderful breakfast spread out by the pool, so I took advantage of it! As I ate, I watched the little children splash about in the kiddies' pool without a care. The cool water splattered my feet from time to time and helped offset the already rising heat of the day. After the morning meal, my sister Faith and her boyfriend who owned an island tour company arranged a day trip around the island for the entire family. My children had not seen some of the key places on the island, and I looked forward to pointing them out.

Our first stop was to the natural tourist attraction, Harrisons Cave. We rode an electric tram through the cave that had been discovered in the 1700s. We heard the calming sounds of dripping water and saw breathtaking views of stalactites and stalagmites protruding from the cave's ceiling, walls and floors. These natural formations resulting from the precipitation of mineralized water looked remarkably like ice sculptures shaped into inverted cones of different lengths. Crystal-clear running water created beautiful waterfalls that formed deep emerald pools. The tram stopped long enough for us to take pictures to help us remember this special place.

After leaving the cave, we drove along the eastern coastline, taking in views of the different landscapes and beaches before stopping for lunch. Along the way, Faith discussed key landmarks that were particularly relevant to our families, such as the home where our family members were raised, the church where Benton and I were married and the beach where he and I had spent our honeymoon.

When it was time to take a lunch break, we stopped at a tourist restaurant that served all the local delicacies, including particular favorites such jam puffs, currant rolls, coconut turnover pastries and ham cutters (the meat version of the cheese cutter). After we had our fill, we were back to enjoying the rich views and the warm comforting Barbados breeze that passed through the van's windows as we rolled along some of the winding and more bumpy roads. Other points of interest included an array of vendors who offered beautifully crafted handmade jewelry in a variety of colors and designs, a visit to Bridgetown (the capital of Barbados), as well as Accra and Miami Beach. We were all favorably exhausted by the end of this memorable family outing.

Now that my family had a chance to see the island, they seemed to understand the initial sacrifice it had been to leave all this beauty for an unknown life in America, a life in a land which I had come to know personally as the land of opportunity. We spent the rest of the week resting, visiting and enjoying time at the beach. The weather was sunny but never too hot. The short minutes of warm rain would visit when we least expected and cool the sun's mighty rays, unveiling a more refreshing island breeze.

After several days of island paradise amidst green coconut and mango fruit trees, it was time to return to my regular life and to brave the winter months once again. Faith and her boyfriend were always so kind about transporting us to and from the airport when family visits. Prior to leaving, Faith gave me some snacks she had so generously prepared for the flight, and just like that, we were on the plane returning home.

***

Not long after I took my assigned seat, I closed my eyes and allowed the motion of the plane to lull me into a deep rapid eye movement sleep. It felt like only seconds had flown by before I was virtually back on the island of Barbados in my dreams. I relived all the beautiful experiences during this visit. After three-plus hours it was time to disembark the aircraft. But before gathering my carry-on luggage, I stored this experience in my long term memory bank, a treasury box that only I had the key to unlock and often did as the thought of my loving family brings me great joy.

CHAPTER 19

Journey to the 17ᵗʰ Move

I am with you and will watch over you wherever you go,
and I will bring you back to this land.
I will not leave you until I have done
what I have promised you.

—Genesis 28:15

The breakdown of cartilage, joint inflammation and pain level of the arthritis increased. The joints within my body became very weak and things like opening jars could no longer be taken for granted. Over time this disease spread through my body. After painstaking deliberation, I had surgery replacing both knees at the same time as my doctor encouraged a dual surgery, saying, "You may not want to come back for the other knee to be replaced."

I spent several weeks in a rehabilitation center. The nurses, aides and physical therapist there had an overall professional approach to nursing me back to health. The daily exercise that included predominantly lower body strengthening and flexibility routines were quite grueling initially. Having had a double surgery, I so wanted to click my heels three times and miraculously return home and would have done so, as quick as a blink of the eyes.

As timing had it, a great opportunity relocated Chelsie's family to another city and the recovery process would transition from the rehabilitation center to my daughter Crystal's home. I must say, with friendly, thorough rehab service and daily visits from Crystal, I did not feel that I was alone. This challenging part of my life, however, reminds me that it is so very important for the doctors, nurses and the like to understand that as patients we have a family that cares and is waiting for us to come out in a much better shape than we went in. On my release date, I was elated when my family came to visit with welcome home balloons. It was time to leave. In light of my excitement, the aides wanted to help me pack up my personal items and during that time encouraged me to continue the chore of learning to walk with what I call my bionic metal knees. So I said my goodbyes to the staff and then I was whisked away in a wheelchair toward the exit and into the car for a short drive to continue my recovery at my new place to call home.

With my daughter and son-in-law working and my granddaughters in school, Crystal did all that she could to prepare my breakfast and lunch before heading out each morning. When she was gone, I spent my days reaching out to other sick and shut-in members from church. Although I called to pray for them, it was a phenomenal experience when knowing my situation they would turn around and pray for me as well. One day I received an international phone call to learn that two of my younger sisters, Jennifer and Yasmin, were flying in from Barbados to visit for a month. When I heard this good news I couldn't help but thank God for family. I believe this was indeed a blessing from heaven. I would have thought it an intrusion to ask them to make a sacrifice to help me, but I am so glad they did.

During their stay, together we prepared many of our traditional Bajan dishes. We shared plenty of laughs and an unsurmountable amount of hours catching up, as our typical phone conversations were stunted by the daunting international phone call cost per minute. A month later I was healing well. I could help myself around the house significantly more – it was just in time as my sisters' flight was ready to return them to Barbados. In their absence, Crystal's home now carried a quiet emptiness, until Chelsie came to stay with her for a few weeks. Having more family around is better than not having family at all. This was a good time. Chelsie discussed with me their family plans and welcomed me to rejoin them.

After a year of recovering from surgery, I embarked on my first airplane trip to visit Chelsie in her new home located in the southeast of America. When I checked in at the airport, I had to inform the attendants as to why the alarms would go off while passing through the metal detector. After explaining that I have metal knee replacements, the airport staff were thorough and pulled me aside to double check my person and items, but not without a little humor. We all enjoyed a hearty laugh when an attendant called me the Bionic Woman, a hero type character I watched with my family from time to time on television.

Outside of Florida, I had not visited another southern state until then. On arrival, the visit got off to a good start as the attendants in the airport were friendly and hospitable from the moment I exited the plane. On the drive to Chelsie's home, I marveled at the warm weather that undoubtedly was responsible for the bountiful tree lined streets that were bursting with a forest of green leaves. On arrival to Chelsie's immaculately clean and attractively decorated home, I was welcomed with ivory, pastel pink and avocado tones that were interestingly intertwined with accents of Aztec framed art and pillows. The upper level, where she had arranged the large guest room, was decorated with my pink floral curtains and matching ruffle-trimmed comforter and pillow bed set. I felt right at home. Peering into the room, I quickly assessed that this nicely-sized space would suit my needs just fine. With a good eye for decorating, I envisioned precisely where my oak bedroom set, that was then safely tucked away in public storage, would be positioned.

To say the least, moving yet again had been the furthest thing from my thoughts, but then the idea of taking my aching joints to a warmer climate brought a glimpse of promise, and a move started to sound like a pretty good concept. Except for the effort of the actual move, it would probably be good for me in the long run. I knew Chelsie would take care of me, so I really had no reason to worry. With this awakening, boxes would again need to be packed, dishes stacked, and glasses wrapped in old newspaper. At that crossroad in life, I should have been considered a professional mover. Instead, moving was getting a bit harder to face at my age. I will miss spending time with Crystal and baking cookies and helping with my beautiful granddaughters .

It is a grandmother's pleasure to spoil her grandchildren with love. Noticing a smile on any one of my grandchildren's faces when I had made their favorite treats, such as my homemade, frosting glazed cupcakes, was always a matchless joy. To hear their delightful laughter when I'd read them a silly story brought such joy. To share a hug or wipe away their innocent tears was well-received at bedtime when we said goodnight with a heartfelt prayer. I wished that all my children and grandchildren could have lived in the same area, but regrettably this was not to be.

I enjoyed helping Chelsie and her family, but after a few years I had an onset of hip pain. Climbing the stairs to my second floor bed-room became a challenge. I began to feel the need to move to my own apartment, but this time when I moved it was to a senior apart-ment building, just 20 minutes from my daughter's home. This build-ing was quaint and decorated with a country charm. I made friends with others my age and as a non-driver enjoyed the convenience of taking the senior citizens' bus to the supermarket and doctors' ap-pointments. Later my hip pain evolved into a need for a hip replace-ment. I no longer healed as rapidly as those my age, yet the surgery went well. It was very difficult during the recovery period but in it all I didn't give up faith. Looking back, I relish the memory of feeling pure joy when I received multiple visitations from church members. These visits were particularly meaningful as I was a transplant from another state with no long standing relationships in the south. I saw the love that can only come from God through the hearts of members who visited me in the hospital and the rehabilitation center.

On this one occasion, after a soft, meaningful prayer for a smooth recovery, just a few family and visiting church members gathered. Be-fore we knew it, traditional spiritual hymns such as "Amazing Grace" filled the air with melodic sounds of hope. The positive spiritual songs drew the attention of other patients and employees who stood in the hallway outside of my room for a moment, just to listen in or sing along. In that trial, I believe God was faithful and I healed well and returned home where I received in-home physical therapy. I enjoyed having a space to call my own. By living in a senior community, I eventually came to appreciate the feeling of regained independence. The move would work for all to be a good idea.

***

After a few years, I was to undergo my seventeenth and final move. Suddenly, there I was again, surrounded by boxes, tape, newspaper and plastic bags, trying to prepare all my personal items for another move. Chelsie found a brand new senior apartment development just minutes away from her residence and the family's local church. On a retiree's income, the less-competitive cost of rent was especially attractive. I would be the first tenant in this apartment which boasted many modern touches like an onsite gym and laundry room and conveniences of physical assistance, such as a metal railing to aide in my stepping in and out of the tub. The eat-in kitchen was equipped with a microwave, dishwasher and large refrigerator. The bedroom was average with a reasonably sized walk-in closet that could stand three to four people simultaneously.

It was also refreshing as the apartment was conveniently located on the first floor. I was fairly sure that this was my last move. I rejoiced that the apartment did not have stairs and communicated to Chelsie that her thoughtfulness was appreciated. The only downside to this new location was a psychological one. It was heartbreaking to see the more senior residents moving in and walking about with canes and in wheelchairs. Some would eventually show to be lonely as they had visitation from their family only on their birthdays and holidays. I quickly made friends within the complex. It seemed as if I was the most outgoing of the bunch at the time, and I made an effort to include neighbors during the different holidays, such as Valentine's Day, by sending greeting cards and baking extra treats to share.

After a lively time which seemed to swirl by as swift as a tornado, unsympathetically, a disheartening motionless time followed as I visited some of the sick and shut in one by one. There was always a disconsolate atmosphere when a tenant passed away. As bad news tends to travel quickly, soon there was chatter in the hallway about the rate of fatalities in the apartment building. Each fresh loss of another friend brought the reality closer to home that one day time would cease. Less and less did I enjoy being reminded of it.

Over time, I settled into the community activities of our local church. Just as with my home church in Brooklyn, the pastor and his wife and others adopted me as if I were their own mother. I adored the responsibility to pray for others, and it was not unusual for someone to reach out to me after church, at my home or on the phone. On occasion, I would be asked for advice about what steps the inquiring person should take to resolve their problems. It is such a peaceful experience to be valued and be able to help someone along this Christian journey. Having more time for reflection, I would often think back to when I first came to New York and about the friends who had supported and guided me. I was so desperate for help when I arrived to a new country. I was overjoyed to be able to give back to life what was so kindly given to me.

In my opinion, there are few things as important as being well and able enough to help a person in need and then actually do it. Like with my own past experience, there may be someone who feels like they have reached their last stop on the train ride of life and who is considering suicide. I often pray for those who are less fortunate and reach back to help someone else.

CHAPTER 20

Forgiveness

For if you forgive other people when they sin against you,
your heavenly Father will also forgive you.

—Matthew 6:14

Each year I look forward to the Christmas holiday, the time of year when all my family comes to visit and to celebrate not only the birth of Christ but also Crystal's and my Christmas birthdays. Decorations and melodies of Christmas carols add to the cheer. Wreaths are placed on the door and over the fireplace. In the corner of the family room, a fragrant seven-foot-tall fir tree trimmed with garlands, lights and special Christmas ornaments we have saved through the years illuminates the living room. Beneath the tree, large bows and cascading ribbons adorn tall stacks of presents. Familiar holiday fragrances of sweet potato pie topped with baked-on marsh-mallows and cherry topped cheesecake fill the air, along with the smell of warm chocolate chip cookies and traditional desserts like the sliceable Barbadian coconut pone. Made with flour, coconuts, and raisins and flavored with vanilla essence, pone has a more solid pud-ding consistency than its cousin the coconut bread, which has a bit more of a sugar glazed finish and crumbles if cut thin enough. A warmed piece of pone à la mode is my favorite holiday dessert.

We definitely eat well when we get together for Christmas! Our Bajan American holiday menu includes roasted pork, a large stuffed turkey, stewed chicken, a honey and pineapple glazed ham, curry lamb, baked macaroni and cheese, pigeon peas and rice, lasagna, a sautéed and steamed medley of vegetables, complemented with a large garden salad.

However, 2002 would be somewhat of a different year. Benton Sr. had called and insisted that he wanted to spend Christmas with all his children and grandchildren. I had never refused Benton's visits through the years, but they had not fallen at Christmas until this point. This was a special time for the family and we birthday girls. It is always the highlight of my year, and I honestly would rather he not be present, so I spoke up and expressed my apprehension.

"Margaret, I understand," he replied, "but I would really like to see all the grandchildren for Christmas. Chelsie has a beautiful baby girl, the last of our grandchildren to be born and this will give me a chance to see her. I really would like to spend some time with them all."

"Where would you stay?"

"Well, I can always stay at your place," he said with his natural jovial charm.

"No way!"

"Technically in the eyes of God we are still married. I promise I will behave myself."

"No way."

"Okay. I am sure there is a hotel nearby where I can stay."

"Crystal and her family are driving from New Jersey, and Chelsie's house is being remodeled."

"Margaret, thank you for your concern, but don't be burdened about where I am going to stay," Benton insisted. "I understand it is a last minute request and that arrangements for available sleeping quarters are spoken for. I just want to know that it is okay if I come and spend Christmas with the children," Benton continued insistently.

"Benton, if you want to come for the holidays, that will be fine."

After we said good-bye, a real feeling of disappointment crept into my emotional state of mind and in that moment I prayed that God would give me the strength to forget the past during Benton's visit and to enjoy the season, regardless of his presence at Christmas dinner.

This effort would be my way of keeping the love of Jesus Christ in Christmas.

To be honest, there was something more to my feelings. Even though I no longer thought of Benton in a romantic way, we had spent many years together, and whether I liked it or not, there was still the connection of the children between us. It was no surprises that not once during our phone conversation did Benton acknowledge that Christmas is also my birthday. I don't know why this bothered me, except that it seemed to stir up old feelings of abandonment that I had thought were finally pushed to the back of my mind. Although I had forgiven Benton and clearly moved on, I knew then that God was still working on me in the area of feelings of disappointment.

Through prayer, I would reconnect to the peace of God that passes all understanding. Sometimes I'd start worshiping God with adoration of His astonishing sovereignty. In those moments of worship, I was often reminded of the goodness of the Lord that I've experienced on my journey. I counted God's gracious blessings and was thankful.

In reflection, I stopped and reviewed Benton's life. Benton had actually been quite consistent in his actions throughout the years. He would call to update me with the changes in his life, particularly after things did not work out with his new women. He had approximately three divorces and two breakups that I am aware of. According to Benton, it was never his fault: it was always the conniving ways of his "Eve" that caused the demise of his relationships. With each divorce, he seemed to lose his finances and his career, leaving him to start all over with a new phone number, a different place to live and usually a different job. I believe that when God blessed our marriage that the vows we took were to be *Till death do us part*. I believe that is why none of his other marriages were blessed. Perhaps Benton sensed this, too, because after each breakup, he would call to tell me that he still loved me and wanted to be with me. Having learned from my mistake in this area, each additional time my answer was the same: "No."

After years of taking insulin, Benton became legally blind and finding jobs became very challenging. Two jobs he found involved answering phones in a hotel in Florida. At one point, he worked with a Christian Science church. During this season, to everyone's astonishment, after he stopped taking his diabetes medications for five years he was healed. Doctors were stunned with his recovery and healing in that season. Benton was diagnosed with stable blood sugar during his regular doctors' appointments. He went on to participate on air as a Christian radio personality were he had success with sharing the word of God with people.

After these miraculous years, in time Benton's health took a plunge in the opposite direction. Benton called Crystal and said, "Princess," as he called her, "I don't think I am going to make it out of this situation alive."

In that instance Crystal prayed with her dad and revealed to him that she discerned in her spirt that he would pull through. "Daddy it is not your time to go. You are going to be okay."

Benton said, "Thank you Princess."

Soon after, the Floridian doctors announced to Barbara, who had flown down earlier to be by his side, that Benton's diabetes count was so high that he should be dead. With one final attempt to save his life, the doctors submerged Benton into some sort of detox tank, pulling off a lifesaving phenomenon.

After this time Benton was still considered legally blind and eventually needed the help of a walking stick. Special meals were prepared by the visiting nurse in his town, as his limited vision impaired his ability to see to prepare meals for himself. The good here is that he did not give up his faith in God and his belief in the healing power demonstrated by Jesus, but worked on promoting the book he had successfully written and published, *The Fall of Christian Standards in America.*

Deep in my heart, I did feel sorry for him. With my Christian values, I had prayed that one day his life would turn around. God is merciful.

So, when he arrived during the Christmas of 2002 holiday, I intentionally dismissed the memories of disappointment of Benton's actions that resulted in my bearing the burdens of life and family alone. Instead, I refocused on the love of God experienced through family and friends. Through this act of tried and true faith I experienced a sense of fulfillment and gratefulness that again birthed a peace of mind in me.

To my surprise, Benton had purchased Christmas gifts to present to our children and grandchildren. This was something he had never done before, and I saw it as his way of apologizing to the children, as if the gifts were peace offerings. However small, each child received an item of gold and the grandchildren a toy. At this point in his life, I suspected that he used all the money he had left in the world to purchase these items. Benton apologized during that Christmas visit, in front of the whole family, for the wrong he had done to me personally and also to our children. It was a touching moment, and it was the first time I'd ever seen him stand up and take ownership for his mistakes. I believe his apology was accepted with open arms from everyone in the room.

After Christmas I did not see him again until he was leaving for the airport. He hugged me and thanked me for everything.

"You are a great mother," he told me. "You raised our daughters wonderfully and they've become women of God with lovely families as you prayed for them to be. I am sorry for all the pain I have caused you. Thank you for forgiving me. I am finally at peace. All these years, during the Christmas holidays, I missed the love and laughter with our children each holiday. It was a satisfying experience you have given me this year. For all it's worth, I still love you, Blossom."

I returned to Benton a genuine farewell hug and said goodbye.

***

A month later was Benton's second time in the hospital.

Now, in January 2003, I received a call that Benton had been rushed to the hospital. The doctors wanted to remove his leg but he had refused. I recalled that he had often said he'd rather die than have a body part amputated. During this return to the hospital, the outcome would be different.

The hospital called to say that Benton was dying. Barbara and Crystal took the next available flights they could get. They met at the airport then drove a rental car straight to the hospital. Upon arrival to their father's hospital room, the girls found Benton in a coma. After a few dreadful hours in the waiting room, they heard from the attending doctor that their father had taken his last breath. The doctors then called Barbara and Crystal into the hospital room where Benton lay breathless. Crystal recounted to me that in that moment of quiet sorrow, with waterworks running down from her eyes and past her cheeks to drench her white tear-stained blouse, she encountered an intense moment. After kissing the blank, expressionless face of her father, wrapped in the stillness of time, Crystal looked up and in her mind's eye saw an image of Benton's face looking down at her with a big smile as if to say, *It is okay, I am in a better place.*

I was sad and even cried intimately at the loss of Benton's life. He'd had such potential as his preaching was an encouragement to so many. As my only true love, my life's journey could never be told without his mention. Life is not always a bowl of cherries as can be seen from the authentic situations of two people of faith, whose lives each played out very differently. Truly the rain falls on the just and unjust. I trusted in the word of the Lord that brought hope and joy through God's promise never to leave nor forsake me. I experienced God's love through His believers who brought support and comfort during this time of loss.

Barbara took the lead to plan her father's funeral. Chelsie created the bulletin. Benton was the first immediate family member to die that the grandchildren knew. His body was flown in for a simple and brief funeral. When all the arrangements were finalized, it was time to attend the service. The granddaughters sang "Tomorrow" from the musical *Annie* during the ceremony. I thought it a profound moment when I realized that the songs sung at the funerals of Benton Sr. and Junie (Benton Jr.) were both titled the same, though they were completely different songs. With compassion and composure, Crystal read the poem she wrote named "It's O.K."

> I often wondered why things had to change,
> Your presence was missed, when you finally went away,

I remember the voice from above, penetrating my very
  soul,
As you declared the word of truth, a long, long time ago,
Your wisdom was our laughter, our wisdom was your
  prayer,
But you asked from a distance that only God could hear,
The days grew colder, as we looked for love's return,
Buried by sin and predestination, but covered by His
  blood,
Although you'll never leave again, a vision I did see,
A smile and eyes embossed in light, awaits, shinning down
  on me,
My soul overwhelmed by grace and perfect love,
  penetrates my soul again.

As I listened to Crystal's poetic words I sensed an unmeasurable power and impact that Benton held as a father figure. I then remembered Crystal telling me about Benton's visit to her New Jersey home sometime after the passing of Junie and his close call with death in Florida. I remembered finding his visit to be interesting as it was unexpected. Crystal told me how during the visit, Benton somehow, being legally blind, used his walking stick and made it down the stairs alone and into her kitchen where he found the bottle of olive oil. He then called Crystal to come to the living room. Surprised to hear her father's voice on the first floor, Crystal rushed with concern to her father's beckoning. The story continued that Benton then put on his virtual ministerial hat and prayed for her, saying, "I thought that Junie was going to carry on my name and the ministerial call. God revealed to me that today I am to anoint your head with oil and pass on the mantle to you."

Crystal explained that in the moment she did not know what to say or do with the baton that was passed to her. Her conversation continued when she turned to me and said, "Mommy, I wanted to be just like Jesus in my younger years but never wanted to be a pastor. So I prayed to God and I believe that as I receive clarity, God will use me in unconventional ways to reach people with the good news of love and peace that I have found by trusting in God." She continued, "People may never walk through the doors of the church, but they may come to a play."

At that moment, my faraway thoughts returned to the service when the funeral attendant announced that the conclusion of service would be followed by the burial.

From there, the body was immediately taken to a nearby cemetery for interment. There at the gravesite, a simple word of biblical support was shared by one of my sons-in-law. At the conclusion, the family returned to Chelsie's home and shared an afternoon meal that had been prepared with southern hospitality by a few neighbors and church friends who stopped by to share their condolences. "Thank you," I said with a smile and kept my sorrowful emotions to myself as well as I could.

Eventually the house quieted with a sort of a hollow sound to the air. Exhausted from the events of the day, I sat still for a few minutes and imagined that Benton must have lived with a huge, gaping emptiness in his life. He had all but tossed away his loving family. I sensed that Benton had regained a spark of hope having asked for forgiveness during the Christmas holiday and then could rest in peace.

CHAPTER 21

God's Precious Promises

"Though the mountains be shaken and the hills be removed,
yet my unfailing love for you will not be shaken
nor my covenant of peace be removed," says the LORD,
who has compassion on you.

—Isaiah 54:10

T hrough the ups and downs of my life, I have learned to trust in God's mercy. In retrospect, I can see how all the pieces have come together so far. As I sit at my kitchen table, each day I challenge myself to remember moments of my life. Some days I could sit for hours and just write word after word in crossword puzzles or jot down moment-by-moment experiences. Other days due to the pains of the dreadful aging process, I walk away. I leave lying there undisturbed the pen, paper and teardrops that have rolled down my cheek onto the table. The circle of life has it that my physical ailments compete for first place with strong long term memories of past, and the joy of Jesus's bright hope of eternal life with God in the future.

Yet having been blessed with fifteen-plus additional years of life, my decision not to prematurely end my life was not ineffectual. At age 80, I remain obedient to the still small voice of God that speaks to my heart. Most of the days, I sit in my comfy, black pillow top lift chair. I continue to cry out to God in prayer for mercy and then again turn and thank Him for family, friends and the body of believers.

I find that I have developed the capacity to choose to appreciate my God-given breath, believing wholeheartedly that His grace is sufficient for me. As long as I have breath, I choose, although the aching is brutal at times, to celebrate life with others. As the Bible says, "Love covers a multitude of faults," and as a result of each trial my character has been refined, shaped and molded. I have come to know God to be like a carpenter. He takes His time, slowly removing layers of timeworn wood from my burden-filled journey. He gently sands them away to bring me to a place of reflection on a refined history which reveals a lovingly spirited Mommy Matias who cares deeply for others. I am confident that He will do the same for anyone who has faith in him. God is no respecter of persons. What He has done for me He will do for anyone who believes that Jesus Christ is the Son of the living God.

I believe the scriptures that share that Jesus came to earth to love, heal, forgive and point us back to God. But He didn't stop there. Christ suffered brutal punishments, was found faultless and was crucified on the cross of Calvary anyway. He died, was buried and according to the Bible was resurrected on the third day. But He didn't stop there. Christ appeared to many, including doubting Thomas, before He was seen ascending into heaven. But He did not stop there. He left His comforting Holy Spirit to abide with us. He took the keys of hell and death before His disciples saw Him ascend into heaven. He has gone to prepare a place for all who believe in Him and He sits at the right hand of God the Father, interceding for us all.

In each of my daughters, I see that same molding process. God has been working on them, too, chiseling away the edges formed over time by human existence, to reveal the next generation of lives of faith well lived. I am proud to have lived a purpose-driven life that includes being devoted to my family and to the call of living a steadfast Christ-centered reality.

I'm proud that my children and grandchildren have accepted Christ into their lives. Some have worked in youth ministry, some volunteered within their individual churches and communities, and some are upstanding citizens who work to make a difference in their homes and careers. What a blessing!

As I reflect on moments past and treasure my fleeting present, I can say with confidence that God is for family. I was thrilled that on December 25, 2015, Crystal and I celebrated another Christmas birthday with family. This time we were joined by family from Canada, England, Barbados, Maryland, California, New York and New Jersey. My 80th birthday prayer was that my family and all who can would seek to gain a greater awareness of the omnipresence of God, as I have tried Him and know Him to be a promise keeper and an ever-present help in times of joy and of need.

In this, my last phase of life, I desire to have my family near. My body has taken a licking as I live with multiple frailties. I often try to laugh when I say, "It's not fun getting old," because through it all I have learned to trust in Jesus. Through it all, I learned that "faith is the substance of things hoped for, the evidence of things not seen." Through unnatural moments with my dad, death of loved ones, divorce, and now the vulnerability of the aging process, I endeavor to practice patience (a long-suffering attribute of love) and kindness to others, with a special attention of gratitude to those who are my caregivers. God has brought me this far and I am sure He will not leave me now.

Although the constant discomfort of a laundry list of conditions are lessened somewhat with medication, I am overjoyed and feel extremely blessed to have my family near. I want to see them often, talk to them, listen to them, and remember and share what I can as I can. It's humbling to be applauded for the simpler things in life like acing my crossword puzzles as part of my daily entertainment. And as I desire to continue to live on my own, with the help of family and caregivers, the remainder of my concerns I entrust to my wonderfully caring children, who sincerely take care of the major decisions of my life.

In the depths of my soul I believe in God's precious promise that He will be with me even until the end of the earth. When the doctors and specialists had given up on me because the larger arteries in my right leg had hardened, preventing the effortless flow of life giving blood to my leg and foot, two out of three surgeons recommended amputation, but thank God my family stood with me in prayer. Unexplainably, one doctor became aware of a tool that can drill through the hardening of smaller arteries and had that tool flown in from overseas. Although I was given a slim chance that it would work without damaging the artery, the life-preserving grace of God was amazingly faithful. The surgery was a miraculous success and allowed the flow of blood to my foot once again. Although I use a walker, I am so very grateful to be able to use both my legs to walk.

Rejoicing in the grace of God being manifested in a victorious outcome, I returned home from the hospital to recover in my black, pillow top comfy lift chair that faced the sun-illuminated living room window that framed a tree-bordered parking lot. As I peered into the clear blue sky that reminded me of the warm blue calming waters of Barbados, I praised God for how far I had come by faith. Then I drifted into a state of relaxation, my body slowly heaved and sunk lifelessly into the fabric of the seat and there I experienced the peace of God. I reflected on each family member and prayed for them each by name. I proclaimed to myself that believing that there is a God is indescribable, to the point where the pains of life come face to face with the comforting promise of hope found in the resurrection power of Jesus Christ.

In the end, have I gotten what I wanted out of life, some may ask. The answer is yes. Through faith, I developed hope that empowered me to achieve what I set out to accomplish with family, work and community. In return, the community and my children pour tangibly back into me. My children bore the burdens of life with me. I am thankful to have had a positive impact on them, evidenced by their choosing to believe in the saving grace of Jesus Christ, their taking me into their homes, coming to see about me, taking me on my day-to-day tasks and by honoring me. Although uninvited attributes of time knocked at my life's door more often than anyone would desire, by calling on the name of Jesus through prayer, reading scriptures, singing spiritual songs and fellowshipping with other believers, I persevered. I embody a blessed assurance with full knowledge and experience that the Lord our God has left his comforting Holy Spirit who is just a prayer away. I hold on to God's promises, they brought courage to my sometimes weary soul and are more precious than the finest jewelry. I fought the good fight of faith. Through pain or tears, but I didn't give up hope. God promises that we will reap what we sow if we faint not. The scriptures encouraged me to stay in the race of life. God the Father and the Lord Jesus Christ are at the helm of our existence and so we all have the potential to leave a legacy of a life well lived as we trust in God's promises. With these promises, I decided to choose life, one day at a time. I forgave others and I forgave myself. After doing all I can do, in faith I handed undesired situations over to God and trusted in his prevailing purpose.

There are moments when I could have fallen off the path. I've been honest with my feelings and my experiences, with unforeseen humbling choices. I've now modestly revealed what was once a secret. My hidden past was unveiled in faith so that the truth of the love of God and His tender undervalued mercies would be seen in a brighter light amidst the dark experiences of life. I pray that a contagious level of hope in His unconditional love would spread faster than a virus and would take root in each of our hearts and be shared one with another. I pray that love and forgiveness will continue to be amplified through our choices, shattering the power of unforeseen calamity and the innate selfishness of the human nature that seeks to divide our families and communities. I pray that the adoption of our loving God and one another would build a greater admiration of God's blessings to humanity and simultaneously thrash the schemes of wickedness and doubt. I pray that we would trust that God's grace is sufficient and not lean on our own finite understanding but in all our ways depend on the infinite comforting Holy Spirit. And when we've done all that we can do, I pray that we will stand again in the peace of God and let the joy of the Lord be our special asset.

I have sat in my comfy black pillow top lift chair and with well wishes prayed in advance for those who would one day walk with me through the sands of time. I am overjoyed and am truly thankful that my purpose continues to be fulfilled through the creation of *Promises of Gold* and the legacy I happily leave of a life of faith well lived.

Acknowledgments

I love you, Mom, and I really don't know what I would have done without your unconditional love and support. You have been there for me and I will always remember all you've done and passed on.

To my daughters: thank you for loving me and showing it, especially during Mother's Day celebrations. I honestly am proud of all of the next-generation insight you've shared and how I see the hand of God on your lives. Thank you for taking the time to entertain the effort of relaunching Promises of Gold. You have been a part of the journey from birth and your patience with the artistic process of our home is admirable.

To my husband: your excitement about what God has laid on my heart is forever appreciated. May God's will continue to be done in your life.

To my sisters: thank you for all the love and self-sacrifice you've provided that made Mommy's health journey more livable than it would otherwise have been. When others would have given up faith, you both welcomed God to use you to help Mommy live in her own apartment, fulfilling her desire to have a home to call her own. I love how like Mom, we have unwavering faith in God that is intertwined with how we stick together as family.

Thank you to my editorial team. As editors and copy editors, your efforts in this regard are priceless.

~Carol Hall

About the Author

*Blessed is she who has believed
that the Lord would fulfill his promises to her!*

—Luke 1:45

Carol Hall has been a producer, director, writer and lyricist of family-friendly plays and musicals for over 20 years. She obtained certification with the Commercial Theatre Institute and Eugene O'Neill Theatre Center and is a member of Theater Resources Unlimited and the Dramatist Guild. Founder of Inviting Developments, she provides opportunities to up-and-coming artists, matching them with seasoned professionals, including singers, actors, dancers and technical contributors.

Carol has creatively contributed to and led community drama programs, script readings and illustrated sermons. She initiated, co-wrote and directed theater for church fundraisers at local regional theaters including George Street Playhouse and the Tony Award winning Crossroads Theater. She directed participants for the Act-so NAACP high school theater program and directed plays at New Brunswick H.S. and Triad Theater, New York City. Carol's musical theater collaborations Promises of Gold and Gee, Whiz God Is have been performed off-Broadway at Lambs Theater, elsewhere in the United States, and toured to Guyana, South America.

Her family life is inspired by her father's pastoral traits and through her mother's Christian character. As a young adult, Carol shared the gift of music ministry as a traveling member of the Hezekiah Walker & The Love Fellowship Crusade Grammy Award choir. As children, Carol's daughters thought it funny that she would sing answers to the questions they'd ask her. She still likes to sing while cleaning and doesn't care who can hear. Adventurous and up to try new things, Carol indoor skydives, hikes, gardens, cooks, bicycles and travels.

www.ingramcontent.com/pod-product-compliance
Lightning Source LLC
Chambersburg PA
CBHW060516130626
46553CB00002B/523